# YE KEN NOO!

## A Condensed Biographical Dictionary
## of 1626 Notable Scots
## from the Thirteenth Century

John Geddes, BEM, is a native of Mill of Mey in the parish of Canisbay in the county of Caithness.

He worked for a few years at the trade of meal miller with his father in the Mill of Mey.

Then he spent an eventful life at home and abroad where some of his more exciting exploits included working in airlocks on the salvage of German battleships in Scapa Flow, Orkney, being a soldier and Warrant Officer Instructor at the Scottish Command School, Edinburgh, spending a period in Kenya during the Mau Mau uprising (1953-54), then serving with the Air Ministry Works Directorate on the twenty months evacuation of British Forces from the Suez Canal Zone Base, Egypt (1954-56).

On his return to the UK he was employed for a number of years with the Royal Air Force as a Work Study Officer and Equipment Supply Officer.

Now retired he resides in the little old town of Minchinhampton in the Cotswolds, Gloucestershsire.

# YE KEN NOO!

# A Condensed Biographical Dictionary
## of 1626 Notable Scots
## from the Thirteenth Century

## Compiled by John Geddes

The Pentland Press Ltd
Edinburgh . Cambridge . Durham

© John Geddes 1993
First published in 1993 by
Pentland Press Ltd.
1 Hutton Close
South Church
Durham

ISBN 1 85821 094 1

Typeset in Times by Print Origination (NW) Ltd., Formby, Merseyside
Printed and bound by Antony Rowe Ltd., Chippenham, Wilts SN14 6QA

*For*
*Alex & Nana Cormack*
*in Adelaide*

# SPECIAL NOTE

While the information given in this book has been obtained from what is considered reliable sources and is believed to be correct and given in good faith, the author and publisher regret that they are unable to accept liability for any consequences arising from, or claimed to have arisen from, any real or alleged error contained therein.

# INTRODUCTION

The purpose of this work is to set out in a condensed form and in alphabetical order, noteworthy Scotsmen and women through the ages and to show the powerful influence Scots have made and are still making, world-wide in every field of human endeavour.

The material has been gathered from many hundreds of literary and other sources, and represents many years of research, with careful attention to accuracy. But a work of this nature must, at best, leave much to be desired. Any attempt to cover entirely the vast field of endeavour and achievement by Scots down the ages, must regretfully fall very short of completeness. It may, however, provide a source from which to begin detailed research and evaluation.

# A

ABERCROMBIE, John (1780-1844) of Aberdeen. Philosopher and Physician. In 1830 he published a work on 'Intellectual Application of Logical Methods in Science'. Recognised as the first consulting physician in Scotland.

ABERCROMBIE, Sir Patrick (1878-1957). Architect and town-planner. Author of the *Greater London Plan*.

ABERCROMBY, Sir James, 1st Baron (1776-1858) of Dunfermline. Judge Advocate General, Speaker in the House of Commons (1835-39).

ABERCROMBY, Sir John (1772-1817) of Clackmannanshire. Army General. Distinguished himself in Egypt and France. Captured Mauritius in 1809.

ABERCROMBY, Patrick (c.1656-1716) of Aberdeenshire. Antiquary and historical writer, best known for his *Martial Achievements of the Scots Nation*.

ABERCROMBY, Sir Ralph (1734-1801) of Menstrie, father of Sir John. General in command of the expedition against the French in the West Indies in 1795-96. Defeated Napoleon at the battle of Aboukir Bay. He shares with Sir John Moore the credit for renewing the ancient discipline and military reputation of the British soldier. Victor of the battle of Alexandria.

ABERCROMBY, Sir Robert (1740-1827) of Tullybody. Army General. Served with distinction in North America and Canada.

ABERDEEN, George Hamilton-Gordon 4th Earl of (1784-1860) of Edinburgh. Prime Minister of Britain (1852-55). Foreign Sec. under Wellington (1828-30) and Colonial Sec. under Peel (1841-46).

ABERDEEN, John Campbell Hamilton-Gordon 7th Earl of (1847-1934). Governor-General of Canada (1893-98) and sometime Lord Lieut. of Ireland.

ABERNETHY, James Smart, born 1907 in Fettercairn. Became Legal

Adviser to the Commissioner of Lands and Protector of Labour, North Borneo (1937), Food Controller N. Borneo (1941) and Resident Magistrate Tanganyika in 1949.

ADAM, Alexander (1741-1809) of Forres. Writer and author of *Roman Antiquities* in 1791.

ADAM, Sir Fredrick (1781-1853). Scottish General at Waterloo.

ADAM, James (1730-94) of Kirkcaldy. Architect, brother and partner of Robert.

ADAM, Jean (1730-94) of Greenock. Poetess, best known by her 'There's nae luck aboot the hoose'. Believed to have died in a poorhouse.

ADAM, John of Maryburgh. Architect, brother of Robert.

ADAM, Robert (1728-92) of Kirkcaldy. World famous architect. With his brother James, designed also the furnishings, fittings and the furniture to suit the houses they planned. From the 1750s till his death Robert erected and made alterations to at least 45 country mansions.

ADAM, William (1689-1748) of Maryburgh. Architect father of Robert, James and John aforementioned, whom they called 'Old Stone and Lime'.

ADAMS, James W. L. (1909-) educ. Arbroath and St Andrews. Professor of Education, Queen's Coll., Dundee (1955-). Education Officer (Scotland), BBC (1939-47). RAF Education Service (1942-45).

ADAMS, William George Stewart (1874-1966) of Hamilton. Professor of Political Theory and Institutions, Oxford (1912-33). Sec. to the Prime Minister (1916-19). Lecturer McGill Univ., Canada (1931) and visiting Professor, Univ. of Toronto (1949), and South Africa (1953-57).

AIRLIE, (David L. C. Wolseley Ogilvy) 12th Earl of (1893-) Representative Peer for Scotland (1922-63). A Lord-in-waiting (1926-29). Director Barclay's Bank (1947-63).

AITCHISON, James, born 1899, educ. Glasgow. Professor of Dental Surgery. Examiner in Dental Surgery Univs. of Belfast, Edinburgh, Liverpool and Leeds. Radio Dentist to the BBC. Visiting Professor, Melbourne Univ., Australia and Otago Univ., New Zealand.

AITKEN, John (1839-1919) of Falkirk. Physicist and meteorologist, known for his researches on atmospheric dust, dew, cyclones, etc.

ALEXANDER, Sir James Edward (1803-85). Scottish General in the Crimea (1855-56) and Maori war (1860-62). He was responsible for the preservation of Cleopatra's Needle.

ALEXANDER, Sir William (1567-1640) of Menstrie Castle. Poet and Statesman. Sometime Lieutenant for the plantations of New Scotland (Nova Scotia). Known as the founder of Nova Scotia.

ALISON, Sir Archibald (1826-1907) of Edinburgh. Led the Highland Brigade at Tel-el-Kebir. Wrote a treatise on Army organisation in 1869.

ALLAN, David (1744-96) of Alloa. Artist and historical painter. Sometimes referred to as the 'Scottish Hogarth'.

ALLAN, Douglas Alexr., (1896-1967) of Fife. Director of the Royal Scottish Museum, Edinburgh (1945-1961), Representative, Museums Assoc., to Canada and the USA (1960) and Central Africa (1961). Was Director, City of Liverpool Museums (1929-44).

ALLAN, Janet Laurie, of Strathaven. Appointed Commissioner of the Salvation Army in 1955. Territorial Commander, Salvation Army, Western India (1951-54) and of Southern India (1954-57).

ALLAN, Robert (1774-1841) of Kilbarchan. Poet and songwriter. Was by trade a weaver.

ALLAN, Sir William (1782-1850) of Edinburgh. Historical painter. Appointed Limner to the Queen in Scotland in 1841.

ALLAN, William Nimmo (1896-) of Callander. Appointed Consultant on Irrigation in Sudan in 1947.

ANDERSON, Adam (- died 1846) Professor of Natural Philosophy at St Andrews. Contributed original papers on the measurement of the highest mountains by the barometer.

ANDERSON, Arthur (1792-1868) of Lerwick, Shetland. Pioneer and benefactor, co-founder in 1840 of the world's largest passenger fleet— the P & O Steam Navigation Shipping Company.

ANDERSON, Sir Colin Skelton (1904-) Director of the P & O Steam Nav. Co., and Chairman of many companies (1960-69). Provost of the Royal College of Art (1967-).

ANDERSON, Sir David (1895-1966) of Glasgow. Engineer and Principal, Coll. of Technology, Birmingham (1930-46). Published numerous papers on technical education.

ANDERSON, Sir Duncan (1901-) of Aberdeen. Civil Engineer involved in road, rail, bridge and tunnel construction. Controller, Caribbean Region Colonial Development Corp., (1951-53). Sometime Chairman, British Oxygen Co., and Director BOAC.

ANDERSON, Francis S. (1897-) of Aberdeen. Chairman Bacon Market Council (1964-). Director, British Sugar Corp. Ltd. (1960-64).

Was Director of Fish Supplies, Min. of Food (1943-45). Under-sec. Min. of Food (1946-54) and Chairman, International Wheat Council (1949-59).

ANDERSON, Ian (1891-1970) of Morayshire. Member of London Stock Exchange for 33 years. High Sheriff of Surrey (1942-58). Member of the Queen's Bodyguard for Scotland (The Royal Company of Archers).

ANDERSON, James (1739-1808) of Hermiston, nr. Edinburgh. Writer on political economy and agriculture. Inventor of the 'Scotch Plough'.

ANDERSON, John (1726-96) of Rosneath nr. Dunfermline. Scientist. Author of *Institutes of Physics* (1786). Invented the 'Balloon Post' and a gun which in 1791 he presented to the French National Convention.

ANDERSON, John (1805-56) of Galloway. Missionary and founder of the Free Church Mission, Madras.

ANDERSON, John (1896-) of Beith, Ayrshire. One-time Scientist at the Admiralty Surface Weapons Establishment, Portsmouth.

ANDERSON, Revd John George (1866-1943) of Orkney. Became Archbishop Moosonee and Metropolitan of Ontario in 1940-.

ANDERSON, John Henry (1814-74) of Aberdeenshire. Magician, known as 'The Great Wizard of the North'. Performed in the Adelphi, London, where he caught a bullet fired from a gun.

ANDERSON, Moira of Kirkintilloch. Singer and concert artist. Became known as a singer with the *White Heather Club* TV series. Her own BBC TV series *Moira Sings*, and *Moira in Person* (1973) were popular. She has done several Commonwealth tours. She is married to Dr Stuart MacDonald.

ANDERSON, Rona of Edinburgh. Actress. Appeared in the BBC series *No Wreaths for the General* (1963), *Dr. Finlay's Casebook*, *Dixon of Dock Green*, etc. Her films included *The Prime of Miss Jean Brodie* (1969). She was married to the famous Scottish actor the late Gordon Jackson.

ANDERSON, Thomas (1819-74). Scottish organic chemist, remembered for his discovery of Pyridine.

ANDERSON, William G. Macdonald (1905-) of Dundee. Was Director-General of Works, Air Ministry (1959-63).

ARBUTHNOT, John (1667-1735) of Kincardineshire. Physician and wit. Friend of Pope and Swift. Appointed Physician to the Queen in 1705. Wrote *History of John Bull* (1712) and *The Art of Political Lying*.

ARBUTHNOTT (Robert Keith Arbuthnott) 15th Viscount. Major-General, Chief of Staff, Scottish Command (1948-49). Commander 51st Highland Division (1949-52).

ARMSTRONG, John (1709-79) of Liddesdale. Physician and poet. Appointed in 1746 to the London Soldier's Hospital, and in 1760 Physician to the forces in Germany.

ARMSTRONG of SANDERSTEAD, Baron (Life Peer). William Anderson (1915-80) of Stirling. Official head of the home Civil Service (1960-74). Chairman Midland Bank (1975), Midland and International Bank (1976-80).

ARCHER, William (1856-1924) of Perth. Journalist and dramatic critic. Was instrumental in introducing Ibsen to the British public.

ARGYLL, George John Douglas Campbell, 8th Duke of (1823-1900). Statesman and author. Held the offices of Lord Privy Seal, Postmaster-General and Indian Secretary. His writings include: *The Eastern Question* (1879), *The Reign of Law* (1866), *Primeval Man* (1869), *Philosophy of Belief* (1896) and *Organic Evolution Cross-examined* (1896).

ARNOTT, Neil (1788-1875) of Arbroath. Doctor who became famous as a practical scientist. Prolific writer on natural science. Invented many useful appliances.

ARROL, Sir William, (1839-1913). Construction engineer. Built the Tay, Forth and London Tower bridges.

AYTON of AYTOUN, Sir Robert (1570-1638) of Fifeshire. Poet, studied law in Paris and became Ambassador to the Emperor. Wrote poems in Latin, Greek and French. He is credited with the little poem 'Old Long Syne', which possibly suggested Burns's famous 'Auld Lang Syne'.

AYTOUN, William Edmonstone (1813-65) of Edinburgh. Poet, humorist and Writer to the Signet. His *Lays of the Cavaliers* went into 48 editions.

# B

BAIKIE, William Balfour (1825-64) of Kirkwall, Orkney. Surgeon, explorer, Naturalist and linguist. Opened the navigation of the Niger River. Constructed roads and founded a city state. Translated the Bible into several languages of Central Africa.

BAILIE, Isabel of Hawick. Singer. The only British singer to appear with Toscanini on three occasions. Toured New Zealand, Malaya and S. Africa.

BAILLIE, Matthew (1761-1823) of Shotts. Physician and Anatomist. Wrote the first treatise in English on morbid anatomy (1793).

BAIN, Alexander (1810-77) of Watten, Caithness. Invented the chemical telegraph in 1843. He also invented an electric clock (1851) and a fire alarm system.

BAIN, Alexander (1818-1903) of Aberdeen. Psychologist and writer on mental philosophy.

BAIN, David (1855-1933) of Reay, Caithness. Carriage and wagon superintendent with the Midland Railway (1902-19). Controller of timber supplies, Min. of Munitions (1916-18).

BAIN, Sir Frederick (1889-1950) of Banffshire. Director, Royal Insurance Co., Liverpool and Globe Ins. Co., Chairman Chemical Control Board Min. of Supply (1941-44), Chemical Planning Commission Min. of Production (1943-44).

BAIN, William Alexander (1905-) of Dunbar. Professor of Pharmacology, Univ. of Leeds (1946-47), Press editor British Journal of Pharmocology and Chemotherapy (1953-57).

BAIRD, Sir David (1757-1829) of East Lothian. In 1805-06 he commanded an expedition which successfully wrested the Cape of Good Hope from the Dutch.

BAIRD, John Logie (1888-1946) of Helensburgh. Invented Television. First shown to the public in 1925.

BALFOUR, Sir Andrew (1873-1931) of Edinburgh. Novelist and expert on tropical medicine and public health. Made several important discoveries in protozoology.

BALFOUR, Arthur James (1838-1930) 1st Earl Whittinghame, of E. Lothian. Prime Minister of Gt. Britain (1902-05).

BALFOUR, Sir Isaac Bayley (1853-1922), of Edinburgh. Botanist. Sherardian Professor of Botany at Oxford (1884-88). Elected Fellow of the Royal Society in 1884. Editor of *The Annals of Botany* from 1887.

BALFOUR, John Hutton (1808-84) of Edinburgh. Botanist. Keeper of the Royal Botanic Gardens. Was Dean of the faculty of Medicine in Edinburgh for 30 years.

BALLANTINE, James (1772-1833) of Kelso. Editor and publisher. The first to introduce an improved style of printing into Scotland.

BALLANTINE, James (1808-77) of Edinburgh. Poet and painter. Revived the art of glass painting.

BALLANTYNE, Robert Michael (1825-94) of Edinburgh. Popular writer of books for boys; *The Coral Island, The World of Ice, The Dog Crusoe*, etc.

BANKS, Donald (1921-) Canadian-born Scot. Electrical engineer. Invented and developed the uncannily accurate guidance system which was used in the 'Patriot' defence rocket with great success in the Gulf War in 1991.

BANKS, Sir William (1842-1904) of Edinburgh. Surgeon and professor of anatomy at Univ. Coll., Liverpool. Served on the General Medical Council and on the Council of the Royal College of Surgeons, England.

BANNERMAN, William Burney (1858-1924) of Perthshire. Major-General, Surgeon-General, Madras (1911-18). Elected FRS.

BARCLAY, William (1907-78) of Wick, Caithness. Professor of Divinity and Biblical Criticism, Univ. of Glasgow (1963-). Lecturer and broadcaster.

BARCLAY-ALLARDICE, Capt. Robert (1779-1854) Scottish soldier and sportsman. Walked 1,000 miles in 1,000 consecutive hours in 1809. He was the sponsor and trainer of Tom Cribb, the English prize-fighter who retired unbeaten. Drove a coach non-stop from London to Aberdeen for £1,000 wager.

BARNARD, Lady Anne (1750-1825), daughter of James Lindsay, 5th Earl of Balcarras. Writer. Author of *Auld Robin Gray*.

BARNETSON, Sir William D. Life Peer (1907-) of Edinburgh. Chairman and Managing Director United Newspapers Ltd. (1966-), and Chairman of Reuters Ltd. (1968-).

BARR, Archibald (1855-1931) from near Paisley. Engineer, who with William Stroud founded the firm Barr & Stroud, Scientific instrument makers and pioneers in Naval range finders.

BARR, Robert (1850-1912) of Glasgow. Novelist and journalist. Became the reporter on the *Detroit Free Press* in 1881. He collaborated with Jerome K. Jerome in founding *The Idler*.

BARRIE, Sir James Matthew (1860-1937) of Kirriemuir. Playwright, journalist and author of considerable merit. Creator of *Peter Pan* in 1904. His other works incl. *The Admirable Crichton* (1902) and *Dear Brutus* (1912).

BARTHOLOMEW, John George (1860-1920) of Edinburgh. Map engraver and publisher. Best known for his system of layer colouring of contours.

BARTON, Andrew (-d. 1577) Scottish Naval commander who cleared the Scottish coast of pirates, and in 1506 sent James VI three barrels full of Flemish pirates' heads.

BASSENDYNE, Thomas (-d. 1577) of Edinburgh. Bookseller who in 1556 reprinted the 2nd Geneva version of the New Testament.

BAXTER, James (1886-1964) of Ayrshire. Philosopher and economist. Financial Sec. to the Egyptian Govt. (1925-28). Financial adviser to the Govt. of Siam (1932-35) and to the Govt. of Burma (1937-43). Financial and Economic Expert to the Egyptian Govt. (1943-46).

BAXTER, James Houston (1894-1973) of Glasgow. Prof. of Ecclesiastical History, Univ. of St Andrews (1922-). Sec. of the British Academy Committee on the Dictionary of Mediaeval Latin.

BAXTER, Stanley (1926-) of Glasgow. Award winning actor on stage and TV. His *Big Picture Show* won an award for the best light entertainment programme of 1973, and his *Moving Picture Show* voted best comedy show of 1974 by the Broadcasting Press Guild and Soc. of Films and TV Arts.

BAXTER, William T. (1906-) of Edinburgh. Professor of Accounting, London School of Economics (1947-). Prof. of Accounting, Univ. of Cape Town (1937-).

BEALE, Geoffrey H. (1913-) of Edinburgh. Lecturer and reader in animal genetics in Edinburgh, London and New York.

BEATON, Douglas M. (1901-) of Ross-shire. Surgeon Rear-Admiral. Was Medical Officer in charge, RN Hosp., Plymouth and Command MO, Plymouth (1957-60).

BEATSON, George Stewart (-d. 1874) of Glasgow. Surgeon-General and Principal Medical Officer to the troops in India (1863-).

BEATTIE, Arthur (1914-) of Aberdeen. Professor of Greek. Lecturer on the Classics at Cambridge (1946-51).

BEATTIE, Colin P. (1902-) of Edinburgh. Professor of Bacteriology, Univ. of Sheffield, and in the Royal Faculty of Medicine of Iraq. Director of Govt. Bacteriology Laboratory, Baghdad (1937-46).

BEATTIE, James (1746-1803) of Laurencekirk. Poet and philosophical writer. Best remembered for *The Minstrel* (1st book (1771-) and 2nd book (1774)). Became a friend of Johnson and the poet Gray.

BEATTIE, William (1903-) educ. Jedburgh and Edinburgh. Librarian, National and Library of Scotland (1951-). Chairman, Standing Conference of National and Universal Libraries (1964-).

BEAVERBROOK, (William Maxwell Aitken) 1st Baron (1879-1964). Born in Canada, son of a Scottish Presbyterian Minister. Newspaper tycoon, became a millionaire before he was 30. Best remembered for his service to Britain as Minister of Aircraft Production, the appointment he was given by Churchill in 1940.

BEILBY, Sir George Thomas (1850-1924) of Edinburgh. Industrial chemist. Improved the shale oil distillation and invented a manufacturing process for synthesizing alkaline cyanides. Elected FRS.

BELL, Alexander Graham (1847-1922) of Edinburgh. Went to America where he invented the telephone in 1875-76. Became Professor of Vocal Physiology at Boston Univ. in 1873. He also invented the photo-phone, a device for optically showing sound waves.

BELL, Alexander Melville (1819-1922) of Edinburgh. Teacher of elocution. Practised a system of visible speech, by which deaf-mutes could be taught to speak. Was the father of Alexander Graham Bell.

BELL, Andrew (1753-1832) of St Andrews. Clergyman and philanthropist. While superintendent of an orphanage school in Madras he introduced the system of 'Monitor assistants' which was later universally adopted.

BELL, Sir Charles (1774-1842) of Edinburgh. Anatomist and surgeon. Discovered the function of sensory and motor nerves. Facial paralysis, known as 'Bell's Palsy' is named after him.

BELL, Harry (1899-) of Aberdeen. Sometime adviser with UNESCO delegation, Florence. Produced many papers and articles on literary, historical and educational subjects.

BELL, Henry (1767-1830) of Torphichan Mill, Linlithgow. Pioneer of steam navigation with the 30 ton steamship *Comet*, launched in 1812.

BELL, John (1681-1780) of Stirlingshire. Traveller and physician to Russian and Persian Embassies (1715-18) and to China through Siberia (1719-22).

BELL, Sir John (1782-1876) of Fifeshire. General who distinguished himself in the Peninsular War. From 1828 to 1841 he was Chief Secretary to the Governor of the Cape of Good Hope. He was Lieut.-Governor of Guernsey (1848-52).

BELL, John E. (1886-) of Edinburgh. Vice-Consul at Paris (1911), Boston (1912), Belgian Congo (1913-14), Magellans, Chile (1915-19), Santa Domingo (1920), Bahia, Brazil (1930-32), Basle (1932-34). Consul at Galveston, USA (1920-23), Portland, Oregon (1923-29). Consul General at Cologne (1934-39), Zurich (1939-42) and Strasburg (1945-46).

BELL, John Joy (1871-1934) of Glasgow. Novelist. His *Wee MacGregor* (1902) humorous sketches in Glasgow, sold 250,000 copies.

BELL, Revd Patrick (1799-1869) of Arbroath. Invented a mechanical reaper in 1826. He did not patent his reaper and made no money out of it.

BENNETT, James Gordon (1795-1873) of Keith. Journalist and editor. Issued the first number of the *New York Times* in 1835.

BENNETT, James Gordon (1841-1918) son and successor of James aforementioned. In 1870 he sent Stanley to find Livingstone and with the *Daily Telegraph*, financed Livingstone's Congo Journey (1874-78). He also promoted polar explorations, yachting, motoring and storm warnings.

BENNETT, John (1893-) of Ratho. Major-General, Director of Medicine and Consulting Physician to the Army (1947-51).

BENNETT, Roland A. (1899-) educ. Stornoway and Edinburgh. Major-General, Consulting Physician to the Far East Land Forces (1946-49). Director of Medicine to the Army (1955-59) and Hon. Physician to the Queen (1955-59).

BEVERIDGE, William Henry, 1st Baron (1879-1963). Born of Scottish parents in Rangpur, India. Economist, best remembered as the author of the report on Social Insurance and Allied Services (1942) known as 'The Beveridge Report'.

BILSLAND, Alexander S. Bilsland, 1st Baron of Kinrara (1892-1970) of Glasgow. Sometime Governor of the Bank of Scotland, and Director of the Burma Oil Co. Ltd., and other companies.

BLACK, Adam (1784-1874) of Edinburgh. Publisher. Achieved fame through the purchase of the *Encylopaedia Britannica* in 1872, after Constable's failure, and of Scott's novels from Cadell's representative in 1851.

BLACK, Sir James (1924-) son of a Fife miner. Professor of Analytical Pharmocology. Inventor of beta-blockers which prevent heart attacks, etc. Based in London he has been described as an immensely gifted man. Has had many awards including the 1988 Nobel Prize for Medicine.

BLACK, Joseph (1728-99) of Edinburgh. Chemist. He showed that the causticity of lime and the alkalies is due to the absence of fixed air (carbon dioxide) presence in limestone and the carbonates of the alkalies. His fame rests chiefly in the theory of 'Latent heat' (which he evolved).

BLACK, William (1841-98) of Glasgow. Novelist and journalist. War correspondent during the Austro-Prussian War. He wrote over 30 books.

BLACKIE, John Stuart (1809-95) of Glasgow. Eminent writer, poet and philologist.

BLACKWELL, Alexander (1704-47) of Aberdeen. Adventurer, agriculturist and self-appointed physician. Was beheaded in 1747.

BLAIR, Sir Chandos (1919-) Lieut.-General. Commanded 4th KAR, Uganda (1959-61), GOC 2nd Div. BAOR (1968-70). Governor of Edinburgh Castle (1972-).

BLAIR, Robert (1699-1746) of Edinburgh. Divine and theological writer. Author of *The Grave* (1743, a poem nearly 800 lines long).

BLAIR, Robert (-d. 1828) of Murchiston, nr. Edinburgh. Naval Surgeon. In 1785 was appointed to the newly established Regius Chair of Astronomy at the Univ. of Edinburgh. He was the inventor of fluid-filled achromatic lenses for telescopes.

BLAIR-KERR, William (Mr Justice Blair-Kerr) (1911-) of Dumblane. Director of Weapons and Engineering, Air Ministry (1958-60). On British Defence Staff Washington (1960-63). Ex-Puisne Judge Supreme Court, Hong Kong.

BLAIR-OLIPHANT, David N. K. (1911-) of Blairgowrie. Air Vice-Marshal RAF, Vice President (Air) Ordnance Board (1963-).

BLAKE, George (1893-1961) of Greenock. Novelist and journalist. Became acting editor of *John O' London's Weekly* in 1924 and editor of the *Strand Magazine* in 1928. *The Shipbuilders* (1935) was one of his best novels. Others incl. *The Valiant Heart* (1940), *The Westering Sun* (1946), *The Five Arches (1947) and The Voyage Home* (1952).

BLANE, Sir Gilbert (1749-1834) of Blanefield, Ayrshire. Physician. Sailed with Rodney to the West Indies in 1779 as physician to the Admiral. He later became head of the Navy Medical Board and was instrumental in introducing citrus fruit on board ship to prevent scurvy.

BLYTH, Charles ('Chay'), born 1940 in Hawick. Made the first east/west solo circumnavigation of the world in a sailing vessel. Rowed the Atlantic in 1966 with John Ridgway. Winner of the transatlantic race in 1981.

BOECE, (or Boyce or Boethius) Hector (c.1465-1536) probably born in Dundee. Was first Principal of Aberdeen University. Wrote *History of Scotland to the Accession of James III*, first published in 17 books in Paris in 1527.

BOGLE, George (1746-81) from near Bothwell. British diplomat selected as Envoy to the Lama of Tibet in 1774. The first Briton to cross the Tsanpu in its upper range. Became a personal friend of the Lama.

BOGUE, David (1750-1825) of Coldingham, Berwickshire. Minister and one of the founders of the London Missionary Society. He was also a founder of the British and Foreign Bible Society, and the Religious Trust Society.

BONAR, Horatius (1808-89) of Edinburgh. Minister and hymn writer. 'I heard the voice of Jesus say', and 'I lay my sins on Jesus', his best known hymns.

BONE, Sir David William (1874-1959) of Glasgow. Novelist and seaman. Went to sea at the age of 15 and rose to be Commodore in the Anchor Line. His books inc. *The Brassbounder* (1910), *Broken Stowage* (1915), *Capstan Bars* (1931), *Merchantman Rearmed* (1949) and *Landfall at Sunset* (1955), an autobiography.

BONE, James (1872-1962) of Glasgow. Journalist. London editor of the *Guardian* (1912-45).

BONE, Sir Muirhead (1876-1953) of Glasgow. Architectural draughtsman, etcher and painter. Official artist on land and sea in both World Wars.

BOOTHBY, Lord Robert J. Graham, 1st Baron Boothby of Buchan and Rattry Head, (1900-1986) of Edinburgh. Politician and commentator on public affairs. Was Sec. to the Chancellor (Churchill) (1926-29). President Anglo-Israeli Assoc., and the British Assoc. of Manipulative Medicine, etc.

BOSTON, Thomas (1676-1732) of Duns. Theologian, remembered chiefly for his *Fourfold State* (1720), long recognised as a standard exposition of Calvinistic theology.
BOSWELL, Sir Alexander (1775-1822) of Auchinleck. Printer and songwriter son of James Bothwell. He contributed twelve songs to Thomson's select collection of *Original Scottish Airs*. He died in 1822 following a duel with James Stuart of Dunearn.
BOSWELL, James (1740-95) of Edinburgh. Man of Letters and biographer of Dr Johnson.
BOWERS, Henry (1883-1912) of Greenock. Naval Officer and member of Capt. Scott's ill-fated Antarctic Polar Expedition.
BOWIE, James (c.1790-1836) of Scottish descent, a colonel in the Texas forces and hero of the Alamo. The Bowie knife is named after him, a knife of his own design first used by him in a fight in Mississippi in 1827.
BOYD, Sir John (1891-) of Largs. Brigadier and authority on tropical diseases and bacterial viruses. Hon. Secretary Royal Society of Tropical Diseases.
BOYD, Lachlan M. (1904-) of South Uist. Secretary for African Affairs (1951-55). Minister of Local Government, Uganda (1955-60).
BOYD, Thomas J. L. Stirling (1886-1973) of Edinburgh. Barrister-at-law, Chief Justice, Sarawak (1930-39); Air Ministry (1939-43). Chairman, Works and Traffic Committee, Westminster C.C. (1952-55) and Westminster Health Society (1956-59).
BOYD-ORR, Sir John, 1st Baron (1880-1971) of Kilmaurs, Ayrshire. Physiologist and nutritional expert. Director-General World Food and Agricultural Organization (1945-48). Awarded Nobel prize in 1940.
BRADDOCK, Edward (1695-1755) of Perthshire. General of a command against the French in America in 1755.
BRAID, James (1870-1950) of Earlsferry. Golfer. Was Open champion in 1901, 1905, 1906, 1908 and 1910. *News of the World* tournament winner 1903, 1905, 1907 and 1911.
BRAIDWOOD, James (1800-61). Scottish Superintendent of London Fire Brigade. Was killed in a dockside fire. Braidwood Street is named after him.
BREBNER, Sir Alexander (1883-) of Edinburgh. Under-Secretary at Bihar and Arissa (1919) and Govt. of India (1919-23). Consulting Engineer to India Govt. (1927-29), and Chief Engineer, India (1931-38).

BRECHIN, Sir David (-d. 1321), Lord of Brechin, Angus. Warrior called 'The Flower of Chivalry'.

BREMNER, James (1784-1856) of Keiss, Caithness. Engineer, shipraiser, designer and constructor of harbours. Was mainly responsible and instrumental in refloating the grounded ss *Great Britain* in Dundrum Bay in 1847.

BREWSTER, Sir David (1781-1868) of Jedburgh. Philosopher, physicist and inventor of great scientific attainments. Invented the Kaleidoscope in 1816 and developed the Stereoscope. Made important discoveries on the polarization of light. Founder of the British Association. 'Brewster's Law' bears his name. Elected Fellow of the Royal Society.

BRIDIE, James (pen-name of Osborne Henry Navor), (1888-1951) of Glasgow. Author and dramatist. His first London play was *The Anatomist* (1931). He was for a time Professor of Medicine at Anderson Coll., Glasgow.

BRISBANE, Sir Thomas Makdougall (1773-1860) of Largs. General and astronomer. Governor of New South Wales (1851-60). Brisbane, the capital of Queensland is named after him. He built the first Australian observatory.

BRODIE, George (c.1786-1867) of East Lothian. Historian, remembered for his *History of the British Empire from the Accession of Charles I to the Restoration.*

BRODIE, William (1815-81) of Banff. Sculptor. One of his major works is a statue of Queen Victoria in Windsor Castle.

BROGAN, Denis W. Born 1910 in Rutherglen. Historian. Professor of Political Science at Cambridge and a Fellow at Peterhouse (1939-). Intelligence Officer with the BBC during the Second World War. Published a number of books on American history.

BROTHERSTON, John H. F. (1915-) of Edinburgh. Lecturer on Social and Preventative Medicine, Guy's Hosp., Medical School and London School of Hygiene and Tropical Medicine (1948-51). Physician to the Queen (1965-68).

BROUGHAM, Henry Peter, 1st Baron Brougham and Vaux (1778-1868) of Edinburgh. Law reformer, orator, debator and writer on an incredible variety of subjects, including Mathematical and Physical Science, Metaphysics, History, Theology and Romance. Became Lord Chancellor. The Brougham carriage was named after him.

BROWN A. B. of Edinburgh. In 1870 patented a servo-motor for the hydraulic steering of ships by steam, air or oil.

BROWN, Alexander Crum (1838-1922) of Edinburgh. Chemist who worked on chemical nomenclature and the application of mathematics to chemistry. The rule of substitution of benzine derivatives bears his name. Elected FRS in 1879.

BROWN, Sir Arthur Whitten (1886-1948) of Glasgow. Aviator who with Capt. John Alcock made the first direct crossing of the Atlantic by aeroplane in 1919, in a Vickers Vimy bomber.

BROWN, George (1790-1865) from near Elgin. General who distinguished himself in the Crimea, in the battle of Alma, and at Sebastopol.

BROWN, George, (1818-80) Scots-born Canadian statesman and journalist. Founded the *Toronto Globe* in 1844.

BROWN, George Douglas (1869-1902) of Ochiltree, Ayrshire. Novelist son of a farmer. Best remembered for his novel *The House with the Green Shutters* (1901) which was written under the pseudonym 'George Douglas'.

BROWN, George Mackay (1922-) of Stromness, Orkney. Poet and short story writer. Published his first vol. of poetry *The Storm* in 1954. Short story vols. incl. *A Calendar of Love* (1967) and *A Time to Keep* (1969).

BROWN, John (1722-87) from near Abernethy. Herd-boy and packman who studied philosophy and became a preacher in 1750. He was the author of the *Self Interpreting Bible*.

BROWN, John (1735-88) of Berwickshire. Physician. Founder of the 'Brunonian' system of medicine.

BROWN, John (c.1825-83) of Crathie, Aberdeenshire. For thirty years was Queen Victoria's personal servant and confidant.

BROWN, John of Paisley. About 1840 with William Polson produced a cornflour powder when they were trying to make starch for cloth from maize. Brown and Polson later became part of a world-wide concern with a large range of other food products.

BROWN, Robert (1773-1858) of Montrose. Botanist famed for his discovery of the nucleus of living cells. In 1805 he brought home nearly 40,000 species of plants from Australia. It was his discovery in 1827 of the irregular movement of pollen grains and the physical concept known as 'Brownian motion'. Elected FRS in 1811.

BROWN, Robert (1842-95) of Camster, Caithness. Botanist, geographer and author. Travelled Greenland, subarctic Canada, West Indies and the Barbary States. His books include *The Countries of the World* and *Science for all*.

BROWN, Thomas. Scottish engineer who in 1977 invented a computer-linked 3-D electric eye scanner for viewing inside the human body.

BROWN, Sir William Scott (1890-1968) of Kelso. Secretary to the Board of Revenue (1924-27) and to the Govt. Public Works Dept., Madras (1935-37). Chief Sec. to the Govt. of Madras (1946-47).

BRUCE, Alexander Hugh, 6th Baron Balfour of Burleigh (1849-1921) of Kennet. Statesman, Lord-in-waiting to Queen Victoria. Sec. Board of Trade (1889-92). Described as one of the most outstanding figures of his day in Scottish public life.

BRUCE, Sir David (1855-1931) Melbourne-born Scot. Physician and naturalist. Discovered the causes of Malta fever and sleeping sickness. Elected FRS in 1884.

BRUCE, James (1730-94) of Kinnaird, Stirlingshire. Explorer in Africa. First to find the source of the Blue Nile. Discovered Tississat Falls in 1770. His *Travels to Discover the Source of the Nile* (1790) was published in 5 volumes. Described as a formidable man, Bruce was 6' 4" in height and strong in proportion, had dark red hair and a very loud voice. He died as a result of tripping and falling downstairs when offering his hand to a lady.

BRUCE, Sir John K., (1905-75) Surgeon. Lecturer on surgery in the USA, Canada, Australia, England and Copenhagen. Hon. Surgeon to the Queen in Scotland (1960). He was honoured by many institutions throughout the world.

BRUCE, ROBERT THE (1274-1327) of Lochmaben or Turnberry Castle. King of Scotland. Remembered as Scotland's national hero. His memorable defeat of the English at Bannockburn (1314) was remarkable when by his superior generalship he deprived the enemy of their huge numerical advantage.

BRUCE, Sir William (-d. 1710) of Kinross. Architect Royal to Charles II. Rebuilt Holyrood (1671-79).

BRUCE, William Speirs (1867-1921), of Edinburgh. Naturalist, explorer and lecturer on geography, oceanography and zoology. Leader of the Scottish National Antarctic Expedition (1902-04) when he discovered part of Coats Island. Took part in many polar and other expeditions and surveys in the Antarctic, Waddell Sea and Spitsbergen (1890-1920).

BRUNTON, Sir Thomas Lauder (1844-1916) of Hiltonshill, Roxburghshire. Physician and Pharmacologist. His best known clinical contribution was the introduction of amyl nitrate in the treatment of angina pectoris.

BRYAN, Sir Andrew (1893-) of Lanarkshire. Consulting Mining Engineer. Chief Inspector of Mines (1947-51). Member of the National Coal Board (1951-57).

BRYCE, David (1803-76) of Edinburgh. Architect (Scottish Baronial). Has been described as one of the greatest architects of his age. His honours incl. FRIBA, RSA and Grand Architect for Scotland.

BRYCE, G. Robb, (1921-) of Glasgow? Airman appointed Chief Test Pilot, British Aircraft Corp. in 1960.

BUCHAN, Alastair F., born in 1918. 3rd son of novelist John Buchan, First Baron Tweedsmuir. Prof. of International Relations at Oxford (1972-). In 1958 became first Director of the Institute of Strategic Studies.

BUCHAN, Alexander (1829-1907) of Kinnesswood, nr. Kinross. Meteorologist. Pioneer of the Isobar System.

BUCHAN, John, First Baron Tweedsmuir of Elsfield (1875-1940) of Perth. Author and Statesman. Governor of Canada (1935-40). Best remembered for his novels *Prestor John* (1910) and *The Thirty-nine Steps* (1915).

BUCHAN, Peter (1790-1854) of Peterhead. Printer and ballad collector. His works incl., *Gleanings of Scotch, Irish and English, Scarce Old Ballads* (1825) and *Ancient Ballads and Songs of the North of Scotland* (1828).

BUCHAN, William (1729-1805) of Ancarm, Roxburghshire. Physician. In 1769 he published the first edition of *Domestic Medicine or the Family Physician*, the first of its kind in this country.

BUCHANAN, Francis Hamilton (1762-1879) of Callander, Perthshire. Surgeon, agriculturist, botanist and zoologist. Was founder of India's first zoo. He carried out extensive route surveys across Mysore, Canara and Malabar in 1800, and later in Bengal and Bahar. His last post in India was Superintendent of Calcutta Botanical Gardens. Was a fellow of the Royal Society.

BUCHANAN, George (1506-82) of Killearn. Historian and scholar. Tutor to Mary, Queen of Scots (1562) and to Montaigne and James VI. Described as the most distinguished British humanist of his day, and had a reputation throughout Europe.

BUCHANAN, Sir George (1854-1924). Ambassador to Petrograd (1910-17), and to Rome (1919).

BUCHANAN, James born in Canada (son of Alexr. Buchanan of Bankhill, Stirlingshire) in 1849. Was one of the founders of the Distillers Company Ltd.

BUCHANNAN, Jack (-d. 1957) of Glasgow. Music hall star. Had a string of hit musicals in the West End and Broadway in the Twenties and Thirties. Sometime described as the greatest song and dance performer Britain ever produced. Certainly one of Scotland's great stars.

BURNES, Sir Alexander (1805-41) of Melrose. Soldier and explorer. Entered the services of the East India Co. Explored the North West Provinces. In 1831 went to Lahore on a special mission and later to Kabul. He was assassinated in Afghanistan in 1841.

BURNES, James (1801-62) of Montrose. Sometime Physician-General of Bombay. Elected FRS in 1834. A relation of Robert Burns.

BURNET, Sir James William Alexander (Alastair) (1928-) son of Alexander and Shonaid Burnet of Edinburgh. Broadcaster and ITV news reader (1976-) Editor of *The Economist* (1965-74) and of the *Daily Express* (1974-76). Award winner, Guild of TV Producers and Directors (1966) and Political Broadcaster of the Year Award (1970).

BURNET, Gilbert (1643-1715) of Edinburgh. Historian and Bishop. Between 1679 and 1681 appeared his *History of the Reformation of the Church of England*, for which he received the thanks of Parliament for the first two vols. He settled in Holland for a time where he gained considerable influence of William of Orange, and returned to England with him.

BURNET, Sir John James (1859-1938) of Glasgow. Architect. The north front of the British Museum in London is his work.

BURNET, John (1784-1868) of Fisherrow nr. Edinburgh. Painter and author. *The Greenwich Pensioners* (1837) is regarded as his best painting. He also wrote with authority on art, including *A Practical Treatise upon Painting* (1827)

BURNETT, George (1822-90) Scottish writer on heraldry. His most notable work is his *Exchequer Rolls 1264-1507* (12 vols) at which he worked from 1881 till his death in 1890. In 1866 he held the office of Lyon King of Arms.

BURNETT, Sir William (1779-1861) of Montrose. Sometime Physician-General to the Royal Navy. 'Burnett's Fluid', a strong solution of zinc chloride used as a wood preservative, was named after him.

BURNS, Sir George (1795-1890) of Glasgow. Philanthropist and founder of the Cunard Shipping Company with his brother James.

BURNS, Henry S. Mackenzie (b. 1900-) of Aberdeen. Director of Shell Oil Co. Inc., New York (1947) and of US Petroleum Institute (1947-60).

BURNS, James (1789-1871) of Glasgow. Brother of Sir George and co-founder of the Cunard Shipping Company.

BURNS, Robert (1759-96) of Alloway, near Ayr. Scottish National Bard of world-wide fame. One of the greatest of all writers of love songs. His vitality of expression was extraordinary. His works appear in at least 37 languages, incl. Russian, Chinese and Punjabi.

BURNS, William (b. 1884-) of Montrose. Economic Botanist to the Bombay Govt. (1908), Principal, Poona College of Agriculture (1922-32), Director of Agriculture, Bombay (1932-36) and Agriculture Commissioner to the Govt. of India (1939-45).

BURNS, William (b. 1909-) of Stonehaven. Professor of Physiology, Charing Cross Hospital Medical School (1947-). Member of the Physiological Society, the Ergonomics Research Soc. and the British Assoc. for the Advancement of Science.

BURNS, William C. (1815-68) of Forfarshire. Missionary to China. Universally regarded as having been one of the most devoted missionaries since Apostolic times.

BUSBY, Sir Matthew (Matt Busby) (1910-) of Bellshill, Glasgow. Footballer and football team manager extraordinary. Manager of Manchester United for 25 years, led his team to 5 league titles. Made Freeman of the City of Manchester in 1967.

# C

CADELL, Francis (1822-79) of Cockenzie. Explorer in Australia. Explored the Murray River. He was murdered by his crew.

CAIRD, Edward (1835-1908) of Greenock. Idealist and philosopher. Master of Balliol Coll., Oxford (1893-1907). Best known for his monumental commentary *The Critical Philosophy of Immanual Kent* (1889).

CAIRD, John (1820-98) of Greenock. Brother of Edward. Preacher and writer. His 'Religion in Common Life', preached before Queen Victoria at Crathie in 1855, was said to have been the greatest single sermon of the century.

CAIRNCROSS, Sir Alexander K. (1911-) of Lesmahago. Economist. Master of St Peter's Coll., Oxford (1969-).

CALDER, George (1894-) educated in Edinburgh. Private secretary to successive Parliamentary Under-secretaries of State (1927-33), Undersec. Board of Trade (1946), Directing Staff Imperial Defence College (1948), UK Commissioner British Phosphate Commissioners (1952-64).

CALDER, James (1894-) educated in Glasgow. Judge, Supreme Court and Legal Adviser, Tregganu (1938-39). Chief Sec. to Govt. of North Borneo (1946-53) and Acting Governor N. Borneo (1946-52).

CALDER, James Tait (1794-1864) of Castletown, Caithness. Teacher. Author of *Sketch of the Civil and Traditional History of Caithness from the Tenth Century.*

CALDER, James W. (1914-) of Hamilton. Civil engineer. Chief Inspector of mines and quarries (1970-).

CALDER, Sir Robert (1745-1818) of Muirtown, Morayshire. Admiral. Was Captain of the Fleet at the battle of Cape St Vincent.

CALDWELL, Sir Dick (1909-) of Edinburgh? Surgeon Vice-Admiral. Executive Director Medical Council on Alcoholism. Was Medical Director-General of the Royal Navy (1966-69).

CAMERON, Charles of Glasgow. Chemist who in 1820 invented apparatus for producing soda water.

CAMERON, Charles (c.1740-1812) Scottish architect. In 1779 Empress Catherine invited him to Russia. He decorated the Royal Palace, Tsarskoye Selo, and built a palace at Baturin. In 1800 he was appointed Chief Architect to the Russian Admiralty.

CAMERON, Sir David Young (1865-1945). Etcher and landscape painter.

CAMERON, (Mark) James Walter (1911-85) Scotsman born in France. Journalist and author. Granada award Journalist of the Year (1965), Granada award Foreign Correspondent of the Decade (1965) and Hannan Swaffer award winner for Journalism (1966). His books include *A Touch of the Sun* (1950) *Witness in Vietnam* (1966) and *What a way to run a Tribe* (1968).

CAMERON, John (d. 1446). Bishop of Glasgow and Chancellor of Scotland. In 1424 he was appointed secretary to King James I. Keeper of the Privy Seal (1425) and Keeper of the Great Seal (1427).

CAMERON, Neil, The Lord Cameron of Balhousie (1920-) of Perth. Marshal of the Royal Air Force (Retd.) Asst. Chief of Defence Staff (Policy) in 1968. Senior Air Staff Officer, Air Support Command (1970-76), Chief of Air Staff (1976-77) and Supreme Chief of Defence Staff (1977-79). President of the British Atlantic Committee and Principal of King's Coll., London 1979- .

CAMERON, Roderick D. (1893-) of Inverness-shire. Major-General Director of Medical Services, British Army of the Rhine (1950-53).

CAMERON, Thomas W. R. (1894-) of Glasgow. Became Professor of Parasitology at McGill Univ., Montreal. Produced numerous papers on diseases of animals in relation to man.

CAMERON, Veney Lovett (1844-94). Explorer in Africa. Born in Dorset of Scottish descent. First to cross Africa from east to west.

CAMPBELL, Angus. A Scotsman who in 1889 invented a spindle-type cotton-picking machine.

CAMPBELL, Sir Archibald (1739-91) of Inverneil. General. Sometime Governor of Jamaica and Madras. Buried in Westminster Abbey.

CAMPBELL, Sir Charles (1865-1911) of St Andrews. Vice-Admiral. Distinguished himself in many campaigns.

CAMPBELL, Charles A. (1897-1974) of Glasgow? Emeritus Professor of Logic and Rhetoric, Glasgow Univ. (1961-). Was Professor of Philosophy at the Univ. of North Wales, Bangor (1932).

CAMPBELL, Colin (1687-1757). Helped to found the Swedish East India Company. Was made a Noble of Sweden in 1731.

CAMPBELL, Colin-Baron Clyde (1792-1863) of Glasgow. The son of a carpenter who became a Field-Marshal. Commanded the 'Thin Red Line' at Balaclava. Was Commander in Chief during the Indian Mutiny (1757-58). Is described as the hero of the Indian Mutiny. Made a Freeman of the City of London in 1860.

CAMPBELL, Sir Colin M. 8th Baronet (1925-) of Dunblane. President of the Federation of Kenya Employers (1962-70), Chairman of the Tea Board of Kenya (1961-67) and of the East African Tea Trade Assoc. (1960-63 and 1966-67).

CAMPBELL, Sir David (1889-) of Ayr? Regius Professor of Materia Medica and Therapeutics, Univ. of Aberdeen (1930-59), Dean of the Faculty of Medicine (1932-39) and President of the Medical Council (1949-61).

CAMPBELL, Eric (1870-1917). Actor of Scottish descent who played the bullying heavy in some of Charlie Chaplin's most famous short films in 1916-17: *Easy Street, The Cure, The Adventurer,* etc.

CAMPBELL, Ewen (1897-) of Edinburgh? Chairman Executive Committee, Scottish Red Cross Soc. Governor of Kordofan Province (1938-59).

CAMPBELL, Ian M. (1915-) of Glasgow? Professor of Humanity, Univ. of Edinburgh 1959-. Prof. of Latin, Univ. Coll. of South Wales and Monmouthshire (1954-59).

CAMPBELL, Ian Ross, born of Scottish parents in 1900, educ. Australia. Major-General. Commander of Australian Forces in Korea and Japan (1951-53).

CAMPBELL, John, 1st Baron (1779-1861) of Fifeshire. Legal Biographer, Lord Chief Justice, Lord Chancellor (1859). Inaugurated important legal reforms.

CAMPBELL, John D. Sutherland, 9th Duke of Argyll (1845-1914). Governor-General of Canada (1878-83).

CAMPBELL, of Canna, John Lorne, (1906-) of the Isle of Canna, Inner Hebrides. Folklorist, editor and author. Published many works in Gaelic.

CAMPBELL, John M. (1887-), educ. Edinburgh and Canada. Dental Historian and Surgeon. Published a number of articles and books on Dentistry.

CAMPBELL, Sir Patrick (1773-1841) of Argyllshire. Vice-Admiral,

Commander in Chief at Cape of Good Hope (1834-37).

CAMPBELL, Robert R. (1902-) of Edinburgh. Artist, writer, lecturer and broadcaster on Art. Director of the National Gallery of South Australia (1951-67).

CAMPBELL, Thomas (1777-1844) of Glasgow. Poet of renown. 'Hohenlinden', 'Ye Mariners of England' and 'The Battle of the Baltic' are among the best known of his poems. One of the founders of Univ. Coll., London. He is buried in Westminster Abbey.

CAMPBELL, Thomas (1790-1858) of Edinburgh. Sculptor. Exhibited various works in the Royal Academy, London.

CAMPBELL-BANNERMAN, Sir Henry (1846-1908) of Glasgow. Prime Minister of Great Britain (1905-08).

CARGILL, Donald (1619-81) of Rattray, Perthshire. Minister and Covenanter. Was deprived of his living for opposing the Restoration (1660). Fought at Bothwell Bridge (1679), took part in the Sanquhar Declaration (1680) after which he excommunicated the King at Torwood, Stirling. He was executed in Edinburgh.

CARGILL, Dame Helen W. of Edinburgh. Air Commandant. Matron-in-Chief Princess Mary's RAF Nursing Service (1948-52).

CARLILE, Wilson (1847-1942), born at Brixton, of Scottish descent. Founder of the Westminster Mission from which the Church Army developed.

CARLYLE, Thomas (1795-1881) of Ecclefechan. Writer, essayist and lecturer. Sometime described as a literary genuis of the highest order.

CARMICHAEL, Edward A. (1896-) of Edinburgh. Neurologist. Sometime Director of Neurological Research Unit, London.

CARMICHAEL, Sir John (1920-) of St Andrews? Chairman Sudan Light and Power (1952-54), Financial and Economic Adviser to the Sudan Govt. (1955-59) and Chairman Herring Industry Board (1962-).

CARNEGIE, Andrew (1835-1918) of Dunfermline. Iron and steel industry tycoon and philanthropist. Made his vast fortune in America. Said to have given away £100 million. He is reported as having said that it would be a disgrace to die wealthy.

CARNEGIE, William (Lord Northesk). Admiral, third in command to Nelson at Trafalgar, and later became First Sea Lord. Buried in St Paul's beside Nelson and Collingwood.

CARSTAIRS, George Morrison, (1916-) born in Mussoorie, India of Scottish descent. President of the World Federation of Mental Health (1967-71).

CARSTAIRS, William (1649-1715) of Cathcart. Minister and politician. Friend confidant and adviser of William of Orange. Spent several years intriguing against Charles II and was imprisoned in Edinburgh Castle (1674-79). Later became Chaplain to William of Orange.

CASKIE, Revd Donald C. (-d. 1983) of Islay. Best known as the 'Tartan Pimpernel' for his exploits with the French Resistance in World War II. He helped large numbers of allied servicemen to escape from Nazi-occupied Europe. Was betrayed, arrested and tortured by the Gestapo. Was minister in the Scots Kirk in Paris for 25 years.

CAWTHORN, Sir Terence (1902-) of Aberdeen. Consulting adviser in Otolaryngology to Ministry of Health. Consulting Surgeon, Ear, Nose and Throat Dept. King's Coll. Hosp., London. Clinical Director, Wernher Research Unit on Deafness, Medical Research Council.

CHALMERS, Alexander (1759-1834) of Aberdeen. Biographer and editor. Studied medicine but turned to journalism. Edited newspapers in London and wrote prefaces for new editions of English classics. Famous for his *General Biographical Dictionary* in 32 vols. (1812-17).

CHALMERS, George (1742-1825) of Fochabers, Moray. Antiquary and writer. His great work was *Caledonia*, a history and topographical account of Scotland.

CHALMERS, George Paul (1833-78) of Montrose. Painter who was in early life a surgeon's errand boy and later a ship chandler. His paintings *The Legend* and *A Quiet Cup* are both in Edinburgh National Gallery.

CHALMERS, James (1782-1853) of Arbroath. Bookseller in Dundee who invented adhesive postage stamps in 1834, the round one penny stamp.

CHALMERS, James (1841-1901) of Ardrishaig. Missionary to New Guinea. He was murdered and eaten by Goari Bari islanders.

CHALMERS, Dr Thomas, (1780-1847) of Anstruther, Fife. Preacher, theologian and economist. He began preaching at the age of 19 and became one of the most influential preachers of the nineteenth century. Obtained through his influence, contributions for the erection of 200 churches. He founded the Free Church in 1843.

CHALMERS, William J. (1914-) of Inverness ? Secretary and Director-General, Commonwealth War Graves Commission (1956-).

CHAMBERS, Robert (1802-71) of Peebles. Writer and amateur geologist. Published the first book in English on evolution *Vestages of the National History of Creation* (1844).

CHAMBERS, William (1800-83) of Peebles. Publisher with his brother Robert. Co-founders of the *Chambers' Journal*.

CHEYNE, James (1895-) of Aberdeen ? Administrative Officer in Tanganyika Territory (1918), Provincial Commissioner (1941), Sec. for African Affairs (1948) and Member of Local Govt., Tanganyika Territory (1950-51).

CHISHOLM, Sir A. Robert (1897-) Became Managing Director, Imperial Bank of India.

CHISHOLM, Alexander H. (1890-), born in Victoria of Scottish parents. Chief Editor Australian Encyclopaedia. Adviser on Fauna and Protection to Queensland Govt. President Royal Australian Historical Society.

CHISHOLM, Eric of Glasgow. Composer and Conductor. In 1945 he was appointed Professor of Music at Cape Town.

CHISHOLM, George (1916-) of Bridgeton, Glasgow. Musician and funnyman. Sometime voted Britain's top jazz trombonist.

CHISHOLM, Ronald G. (1910-) of Inverness. British Deputy High Commissioner to Eastern Nigeria (1963). UK Delegate to International Sugar Conference (1953). Deputy High Commissioner for UK in Madras (1957-60).

CHRISTIE, James, (1750-) of Perth. Founder of 'Christies' the world famous fine art auctioneers. Having resigned his commission in the RN he went to London and established his own auctioneering business in Pall Mall in 1766.

CHRISTISON, Sir Robert (1797-1882) of Edinburgh. Toxicologist and physician. Wrote a treatise on poisons in 1828. Appointed Physician to Queen Victoria in 1848.

CLAPPERTON, Hugh (1788-1827) of Annan. Explorer in Africa. Died in his attempt to discover the source of the Nile.

CLAPPERTON, Thomas J. (1879-1962) of Galashiels. Sculptor. *The Bruce* at Edinburgh Castle, *The Border Reiver* in Galashiels, *Bishop Morgan*, Cardiff, and a number of war memorials were his work.

CLARK, Sir Andrew (1826-93) of Wolfhill, near Cupar-Angus. Physician. Described as one of the most distinguished doctors of his day. Physician to London Hospital (1854-). A great authority on lung diseases.

CLARK, George Aitken (1823-73) of Paisley. Threadmaker (in Paisley and America) and philanthropist.

CLARK, James (Jim) (1936-68) of Chirnside, Berwickshire (born in

Kilmany, Fife). Motor racing driver, twice world champion. Considered by many, the greatest of all time Grand Prix drivers. Won 25 G.P. races.

CLARKE, Alexander (1828-1914). Geodesist. Remembered for his work on the principal triangulation of the British Isles, and for his book *Geodesy* (1880).

CLERK, Sir Dugald (1854-1932) of Glasgow. Inventor of the two-stroke motorcycle engine. He was Director of the National Gas Engine Co., and Director of Engineering Research for the Admiralty (1916).

CLERK, John (1728-1812) of Penicuik. Writer on Naval tactics. Published in 1790, fifty copies of his *Essay on Naval Tactics*, and it is believed that Rodney owed his West Indies successes to it.

CLERK-MAXWELL, James (See Maxwell).

CLUNIES-ROSS, John (c.1786-1854) of Weisdale, Shetland. Adventurer, sailor and philosopher. Uncrowned king of Cocos Keeling Islands, given to him about 1827, and his descendants, by Queen Victoria. The islands were sold to Australia in 1978.

CLYDE, W. McCallum (1901-) Professor of English. Became Food Adviser to the Special Commission to SE Asia (1946). Leader of the UK delegation to UNFAO meetings in India, Bangkok, Singapore, Philippines, Indonesia, Tokio and Rangoon.

COATES, Sir Peter (1808-90)  
COATES, Thomas (1809-83) } Brothers. Industrialists. Thread manufacturers.

COCHRANE, Sir Ralph (1895-) of Cults, Aberdeenshire. Air Chief Marshal. Seconded to New Zealand Govt. to advise on air defence. First C in C of RNZAF (1936-39). ADC to the King (1939-40). Held various important appointments in Intelligence and Training in the RAF.

COCHRANE, Thomas, 10th Earl Dundonald (1775-1860) of Annsfields, Lanarkshire. Admiral. Secured the independence of Chile, Peru and Brazil (1819-25).

COCKBURN, (née Rutherford) Alicia or Alison (1713-94) of Fairnalie, Selkirkshire. Poetess remembered for her poem 'The Flowers of the Forest'. A different poem from the lament for Flodden with the same title by Jean Elliot.

COCKBURN, Henry T. (Lord Cockburn) (1779-1854) of Cockpen or Edinburgh. Judge and author. Shared with Jeffrey the leadership of the Bar. A zealous supporter of parliamentary reform.

COLLINS, William (1789-1853) of Eastwood, Renfrewshire. Publisher and founder in 1820 of the famous firm of that name in Glasgow. He was one of the first to publish school textbooks.

COLQUHOUN, Robert (1914-62) of Kilmarnock. Artist. His works are usually presented in colour shades of reds and browns.

COLVILLE, David (1813-97) of Campbelltown. Founder of Colville's Steel Works, Glasgow. In 1879 he built five of the largest Siemens furnaces and at once gained a world-wide reputation. In 1880 he contracted to supply the iron bars for the rebuilding of the Tay bridge.

COMBE, Andrew, (1797-1847) of Edinburgh. Physician, Judge and author of several works on Phrenology and Physiological Science. Physician to Queen Victoria (1838).

COMBE, George (1788-1858) of Edinburgh. Brother of Andrew. Eminent philosopher and author who first introduced Phrenology to Britain. His chief work was *The Constitution of Man* (1828).

COMFORT, Charles F. (1900-) of Edinburgh. Artist and author. Director of the National Galleries of Canada (1959-).

CONAN DOYLE, Sir Arthur (1859-1930) of Edinburgh. Novelist and writer of detective stories and historical romances. Originator of 'Sherlock Holmes'. He was a spiritualist.

CONAN DOYLE, Dame Jean, daughter of Sir Arthur. Appointed Director of the Women's Royal Air Force in 1963.

CONNERY, Sean (1930-) of Edinburgh. Actor. Star of many great films in the personification of James Bond the Ian Fleming character. Won an Oscar for his part as a Cop in *The Untouchables*. In 1990 was voted the world's no. 1 sex symbol.

COSNSTABLE, Archibald (1774-1827) of Carnbee, Fife. Publisher. In 1812 he purchased the copyright of the *Encyclopaedia Britannica* for over £13,000.

CONWAY, Hugh G. (1914-) of Edinburgh. Managing Director, Rolls Royce Bristol Engine Div. (1964-70). Director of Rolls Royce Ltd. (1966-71).

COOK, Capt. James (1728-79) born at Marton, Yorkshire, son of a Scottish (Roxburgh) farm labourer. Naval officer, explorer and scientific navigator. Charted the East coast of Australia and named it New South Wales. He mapped much of the Southern Hemisphere and discovered the Sandwich (Hawaiian) Islands where he was killed.

CORBETT, Ronnie (1930-) of Edinburgh. Actor and comedian. Became popular in *No that's me over here* and the TV series with

Ronnie Barker *The Two Ronnies.*

COUTTS, Frederick (1899-) of Aberdeenshire. General of the Salvation Army (1963-69).

COUTTS, Thomas (1735-1822) of Edinburgh. Banker. Founder of the London Banking House of Coutts & Co., with his brother James.

COWAN, Andrew, Scottish border farmer and motor rally driver. Twice winner (1969 & 1977) of the London to Sydney marathon rally.

CRAIG, William S.R. (1903-) Professor of Paediatrics and Child Health, Univ. of Leeds. Produced various publications on child and adolescent life in health and disease.

CRAIGIE, James (1899-) educated Perth and St Andrews. Member of Scientific Staff, Imperial Cancer Research Fund (1947-64), President Society of American Bacteriologists (1946). Director Mill Hill Laboratories (1949-58).

CRAIGIE, Sir Thomas Alexander (1867-1957) of Dundee. Scholar and Professor of Anglo-Saxon at Oxford (1916-25), of English at Chicago (1925-35). He was joint-editor from 1901 of the *New English Dictionary.*

CRAIK, George Lillie (1798-1866) of Kennoway, Fife. Scholar. In 1849 he became Professor of History and English Literature in Queen's Coll., Belfast. He wrote much on literary history.

CRAM, Alastair L. (Mr Justice Cram) (1909-) educ. Perth and Edinburgh. Appellate Judge Supreme Court of Appeal, Malawi, (1964-68), Governor-General, Malawi (1965). Athlete, traveller and climber in the Alps, (1930-60),   Himalayas (1960), Amazon and Peruvian Andes (1966) and Atlas Mountains (1971).

CRAWFORD, (David R. S. Lindsay) 28th Earl of (1900-) Premier Earl of Scotland. Deputy Governor, Royal Bank of Scotland (1962-). Chairman British Fine Arts Commission (1943-47).

CRAWFORD, Hugh Adam (1898-) of Stirlingshire. Artist and portrait painter. RSA 1958.

CRICHTON, James (1560-82) of Eliock House, Dumfriesshire. Renowned for his gifts of learning and general accomplishments. Could speak twelve languages before he was 20. J.M. Barrie's play *The Admirable Crichton* was based on his character. He was killed in a street brawl in Italy.

CROCKETT, Samuel Rutherford (1860-1914) of Kirkcudbrightshire. Minister and novelist. *The Men of Moss Hags* (1895), *The Grey Man* (1896), *Kit Kennedy* (1899), *The Loves of Miss Anne* (1904) and *The*

*White Plumes of Navarre* (1909) were among his best known works.

CROLL, James (1821-90) of Little Whitefield. nr. Couper Angus. Physicist. Had only an elementary school education, but in science was wholly self-trained. His works include *Climate of Time* (1875) and *The Philosophical Basis of Evolution* (1890).

CROMBIE, George E. (1908-) of Aberdeen. Counsellor and UK High Commissioner, Ottawa (1955-58), British High Commissioner, The Gambia (1965-67).

CROMBIE, Sir Harvey F. (1900-) of Aberdeenshire. Rear-Admiral (Ret.), Senior Officer Minesweepers, N. Russia (1941-43), Director of Minesweeping (1943-46), Flag Officer Scotland and Admiral Superintendent, Rosyth ('51-53).

CRONIN, Archibald Joseph (1896-1981) of Cardross, Dumbartonshire. Doctor, novelist and playwright. His many successes include *Hatter's Castle*; *The Citadel* and *The Keys of the Kingdom*. Creator of the TV serial *Dr Finlay's Casebook*.

CRUDEN, Alexander (1701-70) of Aberdeen. Author and bookseller (in London). Compiled *The Complete Concordance of the Holy Scripture*, the first great reference work in English, that became the basis for later concordances.

CRUICKSHANK, Andrew J. M. (1907-88) of Aberdeen. Actor. Famous for his personification of the Dr Cameron of A. J. Cronin's *Dr Finlay's Casebook*.

CRUICKSHANK, Ernest W. H. (1888-) of Edinburgh. Professor of Physiology, Pekin Union Medical College (1920-24), Patna, India (1926-28) and Halifax, NS (1929-35).

CRUICKSHANK, John (1884-) of Glasgow ? Professor of Bacteriology, Aberdeen Univ. (1926-54). Was adviser on Pathology to the 3rd Army in 1917.

CRUICKSHANK, Martin M. (1888-) of Edinburgh. Ophthalmic Specialist in Northern and Western Commands (1921-31), Professor of Surgery, Madras Medical College, and Senior Surgeon and Superintendent, General Hosp. Madras (1934-40), Brigadier and Consultant Surgeon, Southern Army India (1943).

CRUICKSHANK, Robert (1899-) of Aberdeen. Professor of Preventive Medicine, Univ. of West Indies, Kingston (1966-68). Produced various publications on microbiology and immunology, etc.

CRUM, Walter Ewing (1865-1944) of Renfrewshire. Coptic scholar. FBA (1931).

CULLEN, William (1710-90) of Hamilton, Physician to whom is largely due the recognition of the important part played by the nervous system in health and disease.

CULLEN, William (1867-1948) of Shettleston, Glasgow. Chemist and Metallurgist, expert on explosives and mining. Spent some time in the mines of South Africa.

CUNNINGHAM, Allan (1784-1842) of Dalswinton, Dumfriesshire. Poet and man of letters. His works include *Traditional Tales of the English and Scottish Peasantry* (1822) and *The Songs of Scotland Ancient and Modern* (1825) which contains his famous 'A wet sheet and a flowing sea'.

CUNNINGHAM of HYNDHOPE (Andrew Browne Cunningham) 1st Viscount, (1883-1963) of Edinburgh. Admiral in two world wars. C in C Med. (1939-42 and Feb-Oct. 1943). Naval C in C for the Allied assault on N. Africa 1942. First Sea Lord (1943-46).

CUNNINGHAM, Sir Charles (1906-) of Dundee. Permanent Undersec. of State, Home Office (1957-66), Deputy Chief UK Atomic Energy Auth. (1966-71). Headed Vassel spy inquiry. Chairman Resettlement Board for Ugandan Asians (1972).

CUNNINGHAM, Sir Charles B. (1884-) of Campbelltown. Commissioner of Police, Travancore State (1915-21), Madras (1928) and Inspector-General of Police, Madras (1930-38). Inspector of Constabulary, Home Office (1940-45).

CUNNINGHAM William (1849-1919) of Edinburgh. Economist. Taught history at Cambridge and economics at King's Coll., London.

CUNNINGHAME, Graham Robert Boutine (1852-1936). Author and politician. He travelled widely in South America, Spain and North Africa, about which he wrote many books. Became a Liberal MP (1886-92) and leader of the Nationalist movement in Scotland.

CURRAN, Samuel C. (1912-), educ. Wishaw and Cambridge. Principal, Royal Coll. of Science and Technology, Glasgow (1959-). Chief Scientist, AWRE, Aldermaston (1958-59). An authority on the detection of nuclear radiation. Invented the Scintillation Detector and the modern Proportional Counter.

CURRIE, Finlay (1878-1968) Scottish stage and music hall actor. Made his film debut in 1932 in *The Case of the Frightened Lady*. Appeared in many great films incl. *Treasure Island* (1950), *Quo Vadis* (1951), *Rob Roy* (1953) and *Ben Hur* (1959).

CURRIE, Sir George (1896-) of Banffshire. Vice-Chancellor Univ. of

New Zealand. Principal Research Officer, Council for Scientific and Industrial Research, Australia (1929-39). Published many papers on Scientific research.

CURRIE, James (1756-1805) of Dumfriesshire. Physician. His chief medical work was the able reports on the effects of water on Fibril diseases (1979).

CURRIE, Sir James (1907-) of Glasgow. Commercial Counsellor, Washington (1947). Consul-General Copenhagen, San Paulo and Johannesburg (1952-62).

CURRIE, Robert A. (1905-) of Glasgow. Rear-Admiral (Ret.). Director RN Staff Coll. (1951-52). Chief of Staff to Chairman British Service Mission, Washington (1954-57).

CUTHBERT, Sir John (1902) of Glasgow. Vice-Admiral. Commanded HMS *Glasgow* (1942), *Ajax* (1944-46), *Vengeance* (1949-50). Flag Officer Flotillas, Home Fleet (1953-54). Flag Officer Scotland (1956-58).

CUTHBERTSON, Sir David (1900-) of Kilmarnock. Consultant Director, Bureau of Animal Nutrition (1945-65). Hon. Consultant in Physiology and Nutrition to the Army (1956-65). Published many papers on physiology of protein nutrition and metabolism, etc.

CUTHBERTSON, Iain (1930-) of Glasgow. Actor. His films include *Up the Chastity Belt*, *Tom Brown's Schooldays* (TV), *Budgie* (TV series), *Scotch on the Rocks* (TV) and *Sutherland's Law* (TV series).

# D

DAICHES, David (1912-) of Edinburgh. Professor of English, Univ. of Sussex (1961-), at Cornell Univ., USA (1946-51). Lecturer on English at Cambridge (1951-61). Dean of the School of English Studies (1961-68).

DALGETTY, James S. (1907-). Became Senior Legal Draftsman to the Govt. of Nyasaland in 1962.

DALHOUSIE, (James Andrew Broun-Ramsay) Marquis of (1812-60) of Dalhousie Castle. Became the greatest of Indian Proconsuls. Appointed Governor-General of India in 1848, the youngest Viceroy ever, and his administration was a tremendous success.

DALRYMPLE, Alexander (1737-1801) of Musselburgh. Hydrographer of the East India Co. (1779-) and to the Admiralty in 1795.

DALRYMPLE-HAMILTON, Sir Frederick H. G. (1890-) of Girvin. Vice-Admiral Malta and Flag Officer, Central Mediterranean Fleet (1945-46). Admiral. Joint Services Mission, Washington D.C. (1948-50).

DALYELL, Tam (1599-1685). Defeated the Covenanters at Rullion Green in 1666. Became a General in the Russian Army. The Royal Scots Greys Regiment was raised by him in 1681.

DAVIDSON, Charles F. (1911-) of Monifieth. Professor of Geology, Univ. of St Andrews (1955-). Chief Geologist to the British Atomic Energy Organisation (1942-55).

DAVIDSON, Revd D. (1781-1858) of Wick, Caithness. Theologian and editor. Compiler of several Biblical Dictionaries and Commentaries.

DAVIDSON, Francis (1905-) of Nairn. Finance Officer, Singapore High Commission, London. Sometime Accountant-General to Nigeria.

DAVIDSON, J. Norman (1911-) of Edinburgh. Professor of Biochemistry, Univ. of London, St Thomas's Hosp., (1946-47). Guest Lecturer to Ghent, Brussels, Brazil and Malaysia (1954-63) also to Oslo, Upsala, USA, Warsaw and Moscow.

DAVIDSON, John (1858-1909) of Barrhead, Renfrewshire. Writer, poet and dramatist. His poems included two series of *Fleet Street Eclogues* (1893 and 1896) for which he won critical acclaim.

DAVIDSON, John C. Campbell, Viscount. (1889-) of Aberdeen. Secretary of State for the Colonies (1910), Parliamentary Sec. to the Admiralty (1924-27), Chairman Unionist Party (1927-30). Controller of Production (1941).

DAVIDSON, Randall Thomas (Lord Davidson of Lambeth) (1848-1930) of Edinburgh. 96th Archbishop of Canterbury (1903-28).

DAVIDSON, Robert (1804-99) of Aberdeen. Described as father of the electric locomotive. Constructed a two-person carriage in 1839, and a locomotive capable of drawing 5 tons at 4 mph in 1842.

DAVIDSON, Roger A. McLaren (1900-) of Perthshire. In the Colonial Education Service, he was Inspector-General of Education, Nigeria (1951-53).

DAVIDSON, Thomas (1840-1900) of Deer, Aberdeenshire. Philosopher, lecturer and writer on Mediaeval Philosophy, Education and Art. In 1883 he founded the 'Fellowship of the New Life', from which the Fabian Society developed.

DAWSON, John A. (1910-) of Aberdeen. Air Ministry Chief Engineer, Coastal Command Air Defence of Gt. Britain. Director of Works A.M. (1940-48). Chief Resident Engineer London Airport (1948-54).

DENT, Alan H. (1905-) of Ayrshire. Author, critic, journalist and broadcaster. Lectured on fine art criticism at Toronto, Boston, Vassar, Princeton and New York Universities.

DEWAR, Sir James (1842-1923) of Kincardine-on-Forth. Professor at Cambridge. Invented the vacuum flask, discovered cordite, jointly with Sir Frederick Abel. Liquified and froze many gases, including oxygen.

DEWAR, Kenneth G. B. (1879-1964) of Edinburgh? Vice-Admiral, Deputy Director Naval Intelligence Div. (1925-27). Commanded HMS *Royal Oak* and *Tiger* (1928-29).

DEWAR, Robert J. (1923-) of Glasgow. Chief Conservator of Forests, Nyasaland (1955-60). Director of Forestry and Game, Malawi (1960-64).

DICK, Robert (1811-66) of Tullybody, Clackmannanshire. A baker in Thurso from 1830. Self-taught geologist and botanist.

DICK, Thomas (1774-1857) from near Dundee. Minister and scientist whose astronomical writings tended to support Christian teaching.

DINWIDDIE, Robert (1693-1770). His actual place of birth in Scotland is not certain. Governor of Virginia (1752-58).

DONALD, William (1891-) of Aberdeen. President The Port Line Ltd., Deputy Chairman Cunard White Star Line Ltd., Cunard Steamship Co. Ltd., Midland Bank Ltd., Director Cunard House Ltd., and Clydesdale and North of Scotland Bank Ltd., etc.

DONALDSON, David A. (1916-). Scottish artist with paintings in private collections in America and Europe. His sitters have included the Queen.

DOUGALL, Neil (1776-1862) of Greenock. Poet and musical composer. Composed about 100 psalm and hymn tunes including 'Kilmarnock'.

DOUGLAS, Francis C. R. (Douglas of Barloch) 1st Baron, (1889-) of Glasgow? Chairman House of Commons and of Standing Committees (1946-46), of Estimates Comm. (1945-46) of Finance Comms. of LCC (1940-46). Governor and C in C Malta (1946-49).

DOUGLAS, Charles P. (1921-) of Ayr. Professor of Obstetrics and Gynaecology at the Royal Free School of Medicine, London (1865-). Was Senior Lecturer at the Univ. of West Indies (1959-65).

DOUGLAS, David (1798-1834) of Scone. Botanical traveller in North America. Discovered many new species of flora and introduced to Britain many trees and herbaceous plants, including the Douglas Fir which bears his name.

DOUGLAS, Gavin 5th Earl of Angus (c.1449-1514). Educated at St Andrews. Poet, nicknamed 'Bell the Cat' from the lead he took against Cochrane of Lauder. He filled the highest offices of State and added largely to the family possessions.

DOUGLAS, Sir James (1803-77). Scottish Canadian fur trader who became known as the 'Father of British Columbia'.

DOUGLAS, Sir James de, Lord of Douglas (1286-c.1330). He was Robert Bruce's greatest captain in his struggles against the English. After Bruce died, Douglas took Bruce's heart on a pilgrimage to Jerusalem and died crusading in Spain.

DOUGLAS, John Sholto, 9th Marquess of Queensbury (1844-1900). Gave his name and patronage to the rules of boxing which had been drafted by John Chambers.

DOUGLAS, Norman (1868-1952). Australian born Scot. Novelist and travel writer. *South Wind* is one of his best known works.
DOUGLAS, William Sholto, 1st Baron Douglas of Kirtleside (1893-1969). Marshal of the Royal Air Force. Chairman of British European Airways (1949-64).
DOUGLAS-HOME, Alexander (Alec) Frederick, Lord Home of the Hirsel. (1903-) of Berwickshire. Parliamentarian. Foreign Secretary (1960-63), Prime Minister of Great Britain (1963-64).
DOWDING, Hugh C. T. 1st Baron (1882-1970) of Moffat. Air Chief Marshal, Royal Air Force. Chief of Fighter Command in the 'Battle of Britain'.
DOWNIE, John Alexander (1847-1907) of Edinburgh. Minister and faith healer, calling himself 'Elijah the Restorer'. Founded, near Chicago, the prosperous industrial and banking community called 'Zion City'.
DRENNAN, Alexander M. (1884-) of Helensburgh. Professor of Pathology, Otago Univ., Dunedin (1914-28) and Queen's Coll., Belfast (1928-31).
DREVER, James (1910-) of Edinburgh? Professor and lecturer on Psychology and Philosophy, King's Coll., Newcastle upon Tyne (1938-41), Royal Navy (1941-45), President Brit. Psychological Society (1960-61) and Social Research Council (1965-).
DRUMMOND, Sir Alexander (1901-) of Dundee. Lieut.-General, Director-General Army Medical Services (1956-61).
DRUMMOND, Dame Edith Margaret, of Glasgow? Director of the Women's Royal Naval Service (1964-67).
DRUMMOND, George (1687-1766) of Newton Castle, Blairgowrie. Described as one of the most influential Scots of his time. Was six times Lord Provost of Edinburgh. Edinburgh New Town, the Medical Faculty and the Royal Infirmary all owe their existence to him.
DRUMMOND, Henry (1851-97) of Stirling. Scientist and writer. Made geological surveys on the Rocky Mountains and Central Africa. His chief contribution to literature was his *Natural Law in the Spiritual World* (1883).
DRUMMOND, James Eric, 16th Earl of Perth (1876-1951). First Secretary-General of the League of Nations (1919-32).
DRUMMOND, Thomas (1797-1840) of Edinburgh. Inventor, administrator and statesman. Invented the Drummond Light which depended on heating a block of lime to incandescence in an

oxy-hydrogen flame. It was adapted for lighthouses and later in the theatre where it was known as 'Limelight'. He became Under Sec. for Ireland in 1835.

DRUMMOND, Victoria, of Perth. Became a marine enginer in 1942. For her gallant efforts–when 2nd Engr. on ss *Bonita* in 1942–during a heavy bombing raid, in keeping damaged engines running, the people of Norfolk, Virginia collected and gave her £400, which she later gave to a seaman's charity.

DRUMMOND, William (1585-1649) of Hawthornden, Midlothian. Man of Letters and poet, mainly on political matters. Ben Johnson walked from London to Scotland to pay him tribute.

DUFF, Alexander (1806-78) from near Pitlochry. Ordained first Scottish missionary to India. He wanted to end Hinduism. One of the founders of the University of Calcutta, which is named after him.

DUFF, Sir Mountstuart E. Grant (1829-1906) of Aberdeenshire. Diarist. Was Governor of Madras until 1886. Elected FRS.

DUFF, Sir Robert William (1835-95) of Banffshire. Man of Letters. Became Governor of New South Wales, Australia.

DUGUID, David Robertson (1888-1973) of Boness. Major-General Engineering. Director of Mechanical Engineering, India, and head of the Corps of Indian Electrical and Mechanical Engineering (1943-46).

DUGUID, John B. (1895-) of Belhevie, Aberdeenshire. Lecturer in Morbid Anatomy and History. Adviser on Histopathology to the Institute for Medical Research, Kuala Lumpur, Malaya (1960-68).

DUKE-ELDER, Sir Stewart, St Andrews' First Foundation Scholar (1915). Ophthalmic surgeon of world renown.

DUNBAR, Claud I. H. (1909-) of Aviemore? Major-General. Commanded 2nd Guards Bde. (1949-50) and 4th Guards Bde. (1950-52). General Officer Commanding Berlin (British Sector) (1962-).

DUNBAR-NASMITH, David (1921-) of Glenrothes. Rear Admiral. Retired in 1972 as Flag Officer, Scotland and Northern Ireland, and several NATO appointments.

DUNCAN, Adam (1731-1804) of Dundee. When admiral in command of the North Sea Fleet he blockaded the Dutch Fleet for two years. Victor of the battle of Camperdown in 1797.

DUNCAN, David (1900-) of Dumfries. Surgeon Rear Admiral. Malariaologist and Hygienist, Singapore (1930-38).     Senior MO, Medical Hygiene Sections and Naval Medical Officer of Health to C in C, Nore (1950-53).   MOH to C in C,  Portsmouth (1953-55).

DUNCAN, Dr Henry (1774-) of Lochrutton nr. Dumfries. Theologian, Antiquarian, Geologist and poet. He established the first Savings Bank in 1810 at Ruthwell.

DUNDAS, David (1735-1820). Scottish General, sometime Commander in Chief, British Army. Described as the profoundest tactician in England. Was responsible for many major reforms in military tactics.

DUNDAS, Henry, 1st Viscount Melville and Baron Dunira (1742-1811). Parliamentarian. Keeper of the Signet for Scotland (1777). As President of the Board of Control under Pitt he introduced a bill for restoring the Scottish estates forfeited after the '45.

DUNDAS, Sir Robert (1881-) of Perthshire. Administration Officer, Nigeria (1911-30).

DUNDEE, John Graham of Claverhouse. 1st Viscount (1649-89). Soldier. Defeated the Covenanters at Bothwell Brig. Known by his friends as 'Bonnie Dundee' and by his enemies as 'Bloody Clavers'.

DUNDONALD, Thomas Cochrane, 10th Earl of Dundonald (1775-1860) of Hamilton. Naval commander with some remarkable achievements in the harassment of enemy coasts and shipping. Advocated steam power for warships. His 'Secret War Plan' (to overwhelm fleets and fortresses by sulphur fumes) was in 1812 and 1846 condemned as too inhumane, though infallable, and was not revealed till 1908 (in Penmure papers).

DUNLOP, John Boyd, (1840-1921) of Dreghorn, Ayrshire. Veterinary surgeon. Invented the pneumatic tyre in 1888.

DUNN, Patrick H. (1912-) of Argylshire. Air Marshal. AOC in C, Flying Training Command (1964-).

DUNNE, J. W. of Perthshire. Man of Letters. In 1907 he tested the first swept-wing tailless biplane at Blair Atholl.

DUNNETT, Alastair (1908-) of Kilmalcolm. Journalist and editor of the *Daily Record* (1946-55) and *Scotsman* (1956-72). He was chief press officer to the Sec. of State for Scotland (1940-46). Director of Scottish TV (1975-79).

DUNNETT, Dorothy (née Halliday) of Dunfermline. Popular novelist wife of Alastair Dunnett. Her book *King Hereafter* (1982) reveals strange new facts about the history of Macbeth. She is also an artist.

DUNNETT, Sir James (1914-) of Edinburgh? Permanent Under-Secretary of State, Ministry of Defence (1966-)

DUNS-SCOTUS, Johannes (c.1265-1308) of Maxton, Roxburgh.

Scholastic and theologian. Became a Franciscan Friar. Theological professor at Oxford, and later, Regent of the Univ. of Paris. It was his name that gave rise to the term 'Dunce'.

DUTHIE, Sir William (1892-) of Portessie, Banffshire. Appointed Area Bread Officer, London and SE England in 1940 and Director Emergency Bread Supplies, Min. of Food in 1941.

DYCE, Alexander (1798-1869) of Edinburgh. Critic and Man of Letters. Edited Peele, Webster, Greene, Shirley, Middleton, Beaumont and Fletcher, Marlowe and Shakespeare.

DYCE, William (1806-64) of Aberdeen. Historical and religious painter. From 1844 was professor of Fine Arts in King's Coll., London. Executed frescoes in the new House of Lords, Osborne House, Buckingham Palace and All Saints.

DYSON, Sir Frank (1868-1939). Astronomer Royal (1910-33). Previously Astronomer Royal for Scotland (1905-10).

# E

EADIE, John (1810-76) of Alva. Theologian and writer. Wrote the *Biblical Cyclopaedia* (1848), and *Ecclesiastical Encyclopaedia* (1861).

EASTON, John Murray (1889-) of Aberdeen. Architect. His buildings include the Royal Horticultural Society Hall, London (1928), the Gillette factory, South Bank Development Scheme, London (1953) and the University of Malaya (1953).

ELGIN, Andrew Douglas A. T. Bruce, 11th Earl of Elgin and Kincardine. Director United Dominions Trust, Dominion Ins. Co. and several other directorships. Grand Master Mason for Scotland (1961-65). Member of HM Bodyguard for Scotland, (The Royal Company of Archers).

ELGIN, Edward James Bruce, 10th Earl of Elgin and Kincardine (1881-1966). Was chairman Standing Council of Scottish Chiefs. Held many directorships in banking and insurance. Chairman Land Settlement Assoc., England and Wales (1933-46), Carnegie UK Trust (1923-46) and Forth Conservancy Board (1926-55).

ELGIN, James Bruce, 8th Earl of Elgin (1811-63). Governor of Jamaica (1842-46), of Canada (1846-54) and of India (1861). Displayed very great administrative ability.

ELGIN, Thomas Bruce, 7th Earl of Elgin (1766-1841). Diplomat and art connoisseur. Was instrumental in the purchase for the nation of sculptures from the ruined Parthenon in Athens, now known as the 'Elgin Marbles'.

ELIOT LOCKHART, Sir Allan (1905-) of Cleghorn. Head of Dept. of Supply, Govt. of India (1940-46), Director-General of Munitions Production (1945-46). President, Assoc. Chamber of Commerce and Bengal Chamber of Commerce and Industry (1951-52).

ELIZABETH, Lady Elizabeth Angela Marguerite Bowes-Lyon of Glamis Castle, nr. Forfar, Angus. Her Majesty Queen Elizabeth the Queen Mother.

ELLIOT, Gilbert, 1st Earl Minto (1751-1814). Governor-General of India (1807-13). One of the greatest of India's Governor-Generals.

ELLIOT, Henry H. (1891-) of Roxburghshire. Lieut.-Colonel, and Surgeon, British Legation, Kabul, (1930-35), Surgeon to the Viceroy (1936-43) and Chief Medical Officer, Baluchistan.

ELLIOT, Jean (1727-1805) of Minto House, Teviotdale. Lyricist. Author of *The Flowers of the Forest*, a lament for Flodden.

ELLIOT, Walter (1888-1958). Politician, writer and broadcaster. Minister of Agriculture (1932-36), Sec. for Scotland (1936-38) and Minister of Health (1938-40).

ELLIOTT, George Augustus, 1st Baron Heathfield of Stobs, Roxburghshire. Soldier and General. When Governor of Gibraltar, he saved the Rock for Britain after four years seige by the French and Spanish forces (1779-83). Ranked as one of the most memorable achievements of British arms.

ELPHINSTONE, George Keith (1746-1823), Viscount Keith of Stirling. Commanded the Naval expedition (1795-97) which took Cape Town, and the fleet which landed Abercromby's army in Aboukir Bay in 1801.

ELPHINSTONE, Sir Keith (1864-1941) of Musselburgh. Engineer, who between 1893 and 1914 was connected with the development and invention of many electrical and mechanical devices. He designed the first chart recorder, and invented the speedometer for motor cars.

ELPHINSTONE, Mountstuart (1779-185?) of Edinburgh? Historian and Statesman. Was one of the founders of Britain's Indian Empire. Governor of Bombay (1819-27). In 1829 he declined the position of Governor-General of India.

ELPHINSTONE, William (1431-1514) of Glasgow? Statesman. Lecturer on law in Paris and Orleans. Ambassador to France under James IV (1491) and keeper of the Privy Seal from 1492. Was responsible for introducing the printing press (Chapman and Miller) into Scotland.

EMERY, Eleanor, of Glasgow. Diplomat. Appointed High Commissioner in Botswana in 1973. Britain's first woman High Commissioner.

ERROL of HALE, Frederick James Elliot (1914-). Engineer. Economic Sec. to the Treasury (1958-59), Minister of State, Board of

Trade (1961-63), Minister of Power (1963-64), and many other important appointments at home and abroad.

ERSKINE of RERRICK, John Maxwell Erskine 1st Baron (1893-1980) of Kircudbright. Governor of Northern Ireland (1964-68). President, Scottish Savings Committee (1948-58). Several chairmanships in banking and commerce.

ERSKINE, Henry (1746-1817) of Edinburgh. Jurist, writer, orator and wit. Became Lord Advocate in 1783, and Dean of the Faculty of Advocates in 1785, but was deposed in 1796 for supporting, at a meeting, a resolution against the Government's Seditious Writings Bill. Was again Lord Advocate in 1806.

ERSKINE, Ralph (1685-1752) probably of Berwickshire. Minister whose sermons were greatly prized, and many of them were translated into Dutch. His *Gospel's Sonnets* and *Scripture Songs* are well known.

ERSKINE, Thomas, 1st Baron (1749-1828) of Edinburgh. Lord Chancellor of England. Called to the Bar in 1778, and his success was immediate and unprecedented. His brilliant defence of Capt. Baillie, Lieut.-Governor of Greenwich Hosp., overwhelmed him with briefs. Successfully defended (1779) Admiral Lord Keppel and in 1781 secured the acquittal of Lord George Gordon.

EWART, James Cosser (1851-1934) of Penicuik nr. Edinburgh. Zoologist. Carried out notable experiments on animal breeding and hybridization, and disproved the theory of telegony. His works incl. *The Development of the Horse* (1915), *Moulting of the King Penguin* (1917) and *The Nesting Feathers of the Mallard* (1921).

EWING, Sir Alexander (1896-) of Edinburgh? Emeritus Professor of Audiology and Education of the Deaf (1944-46) Manchester. Produced many publications on the education and training of deaf children.

EWING, Sir James Alfred (1855-1935) of Dundee. Physicist and Professor of Engineering at Tokyo and Dundee, of Mechanism at Cambridge (1890-1903), and Director of Naval Education (1903-16). In the Great War he was decipherer of intercepted messages. Invented a number of instruments to test magnetic properties.

# F

FAIRBAIRN, Andrew Martin (1834-1912) of Inverkeithing. Theologian, known for his brilliant essays in the *Contemporary review* and his *Studies of the Philosophy of Religion in History* (1876).

FAIRBAIRN, Sir William (1789-1874) of Kelso. Civil and mechanical engineer and inventor. First in the utilisation of iron in shipbuilding. Devised a riveting machine. Built a thousand bridges. Elected FRS in 1850.

FAIRLIE, Robert Francis (1831-85). Scottish engineer and inventor of a railway engine with pivoted driving bogies in 1863, allowing trains to negotiate tighter bends.

FALCONER, Hugh (1808-65) of Forres. Botanist. Made the first experiments in growing tea in India. Became Professor of Botany at Calcutta in 1847.

FALCONER, Ion Keith (1856-87) third son of the Earl of Kintore. Orientalist, missionary and athlete. A keen cyclist, he defeated the then (1878) fastest man in the world. Was Professor of Arabic at Cambridge. Settled at Shaikh Othman, near Aden as a Free Church missionary where he died of a fever.

FALCONER, William (1732-69) of Edinburgh. Poet. Wrote 'The Shipwreck', a stirring poem of his experiences on an East Indiaman.

FARQUHARSON, David (1840-1907) of Blairgowrie. Painter, who specialised in landscapes of the Scottish Highlands and Cornish Coast.

FARQUHARSON, Sir James (1903-) of Angus. Chief Engineer Tanganyika Railways (1941-45) and General Manager (1945-48), and many other important posts in East Africa.

FERGUSON, Adam (1723-1816) of Perthshire. Philosopher and historian. Prof. of Mathematics and Moral Philosophy at Edinburgh Univ. (1764-85). His principal works incl. *Essays on the History of Civil Society* (1765) and *History of the Progress and Termination of the Roman Republic* (1782). Sir Walter Scott was his intimate friend.

FERGUSON, James (1710-76) of Rothiemay, Banffshire. Eminent scientific lecturer, astronomer and portrait painter. Fellow of the Royal Society.

FERGUSON, Patrick (1744-80) of Pitfour, Aberdeenshire. Inventor of a breech-loading rifle. In 1776 he patented his rifle, which was capable of firing seven shots a minute and sighted for ranges 100 to 500 yards.

FERGUSON, Robert (1637-1714) of Alford, Aberdeenshire. Called 'The Plotter', he played, for ten years, a leading role in every treasonable scheme against the last two Stuart kings.

FERGUSON, William A. (1902-) of Glasgow. Secretary British Museum (Natural History) (1959-). Finance Officer, British Museums (1953-59).

FERGUSON, William Gow (c.1632-c.1695). Scottish painter of still life who spent most of his career in the Netherlands.

FERGUSSON, Sir Bernard (1911-). Brigadier and wartime Chindit leader. Director Combined Operations (1945-46). Governor-General of New Zealand (1962-67).

FERGUSSON, Sir Ewan (1897-) of Coatbridge? Chairman and Managing Director, the Straits Trading Co. Ltd., Singapore, 1947-. Chairman, Singapore Chamber of Commerce (1946-53).

FERGUSSON, James (1808-86) of Ayr. Agricultural historian. Compiled the first general history of agriculture. Travelled through India. studied Indian rock temples, wrote on fortifications and archaeology. Author of a popular *History of Architecture* (1865-67), and a book on the use of earthworks in fortifications.

FERGUSSON, Sir James (1832-1907) of Edinburgh. Statesman. Governor of South Australia (1868-73), of New Zealand (1873-74) and of Bombay (1880-85). He perished in the earthquake of 1907 at Kingston, Jamaica.

FERGUSSON, Robert (1750-74) of Edinburgh. Poet, sometimes described as Scotland's second greatest poet. Robert Burns was greatly influenced by his poems which were first published in 1773.

FERGUSSON, Sir William (1808-77) of Prestonpans. Surgeon. President of the Royal College of Surgeons, London (1870-). Elected FRS.

FERRIER, Sir David (1843-1928) of Aberdeen. Neurologist. Joined the staff of King's Coll., London where he was appointed to the specially created Chair of Neurothology in 1887. Best remembered for his work on the localization of brain functions, on which he was ahead of his time.

FERRIER, John (1761-1815) from near Jedburgh. Poet, doctor and critic. At Manchester, where he became a doctor to the Infirmary, he campaigned for better sanitary laws.

FERRIER, Susan Edmonstone (1782-1854) of Edinburgh. Novelist. Her first work *Marriage* (1818) was followed by *The Inheritance* (1824) and by *Destiny* (1831) which was considered her best novel.

FERRIER, Victor, 1st Baron of Culter (life peer) (1900-) of Edinburgh. Sometime Director, Imperial Bank of India, and President, Bombay Chamber of Commerce.

FETTES, Sir William (1750-1836). Founder of Fettes College, Edinburgh.

FIFE, or Phyfe, Sir Duncan. Scottish cabinetmaker who became famous in America.

FINDLATER, Andrew (1810-85) of Aberdour. Editor. Edited the first edition of Chamber's *Encyclopaedia* (1860-68). Wrote manuals on astronomy, philology, physical geography and physiography.

FINDLAY, Alexander (1874-). Professor Emeritus of Chemistry. Was examiner in chemistry at Univ's. of Aberdeen, Durham, London, Wales, St Andrews and New Zealand. Visited India and S. Africa on behalf of the Royal Institute of Chemistry (1947-48).

FINDLAY, Alexander J., (1886-) of Aberdeen. Director of Agriculture, Zanzibar (1931-37). Commissioner for the Colonial Exhibition, World's Fair, New York (1939-40).

FINLAISON, John (1783-1860) of Thurso, Caithness. Government actuary for the National Debt and Chief Government Calculator. He rose to be President of the Institute of Actuaries. His most important work was in helping the Civil Service to organize the establishment of a national system for the registration of births, deaths and marriages, which came in 1837.

FINLAY, Robert B., Viscount Finlay (1842-1929) of Edinburgh. Called to the English Bar in 1867. Became Solicitor-General (1895-1900), Attorney General (1900-06), Lord Chancellor (1916-19) and in 1920, appointed member of the Hague Permanent Court of Arbitration.

FINLAYSON, Horace (1885-1969) of Aberdeen. Professor of Politics and Public Administration, Chinese Govt. Univ., Peking (1910). Technical Adviser to the Bank of Greece under League of Nations Reconstruction Scheme (1828-37). In Intelligence Branch, Ministry of Economic Warfare (1939-45).

FINLAYSON, James, an Ayrshire farmer invented a self-cleaning harrow or grubber in 1820.

FINNISTON, Sir Harold Montague (Monty) (1912-) of Glasgow. Metallurgist. Chairman of the British Steel Corporation (1973-76).

FISHER, Andrew (1862-1929) of Kilmarnock. Prime Minister of Australia (1908-09) and (1910-13).

FLECK, Sir Alexander (1889-1968) of Saltcoats. Industrialist. By 1931 was managing Director of the General Chemical Div. of the Imperial Chemical Industry. During World War II his main responsibility was to maintain supplies of explosives. Became Chairman ICI in 1953. Elected FRS in 1955.

FLEMING, Sir Alexander (1881-1955) of Darvel, Strathclyde. Bacteriologist. Discovered Penicillin in 1928. Elected FRS in 1943. Nobel Prize winner for Medicine in 1945.

FLEMING, John M. (1911-) of Bathgate. Economist. Visiting professor Columbia Univ., New York (1951-54). Adviser, International Monetary Fund (1959) and Deputy Director, Research Dept. International Monetary Fund (1964-).

FLEMING, Margaret (1903-11) of Kirkcaldy. Child author known as Pet Marjorie. She wrote verses and a diary, which were later published.

FLEMING, Sir Sandford (1827-1915) of Kirkcaldy. Canadian engineer. Took a prominent part in railway development in Upper Canada. Chief Engineer, Northern Railways (1855-63). The originator of 'Standard Time'.

FLEMING, Tom (1927-) of Edinburgh. Actor, Director, Poet, Author and radio and TV commentator (since 1952). Gave outstanding performances as an actor in *Jesus of Nazareth* and *An Age of Kings*.

FLETCHER, Andrew (1655-1716) of East Lothian. Statesman and political writer. Opposed the union of the crowns and advocated federation rather than incorporation. Introduced various improvements in agriculture. Was noted for his saying "Give me the making of the songs of a nation, and I care not who makes its laws" which occurs in his *Conversation concerning a Right Regulation of Government for the Common Good of Mankind* (1703).

FORBES, Archibald (1838-1900). Scottish war correspondent for *The Daily News* on the Franco-Russian War, the Carlist revolt, the Russo-Turkish campaign and the Zulu war.

FORBES, Sir Archibald (1903-) of Johnstone, Renfrewshire. Chairman, Midland Bank Ltd. and Midland International Bank Ltd. (1964-).

FORBES, Sir Douglas (1890-) of Aberdeen. Director, National Bank of Australia Ltd. (1948-67).

FORBES, Duncan (1685-1747) of Culloden, Inverness-shire. Advocate. Became Lord President of the Court of Sessions in 1737.

FORBES, Gilbert (1908-) of Glasgow. Regius Professor of Forensic Medicine. Senior Lecturer on Forensic Medicine, Univ. of Sheffield (1948-56). Examiner in Forensic Medicine Univs. of Manchester, Leeds, Glasgow, Aberdeen and Edinburgh.

FORBES, James D. (1809-68) of Edinburgh. Scientist and writer. Was one of the founders of the British Association in 1831. His investigations and discoveries embraced the subjects of heat, light polarization and especially glaciers.

FORBES, Sir John (1787-1861) of Cuttlebrae, Banffshire. Physician. Was joint editor of the *Cyclopaedia of Practical Medicine* (1832-35). Translated the works of Auenbrugger and Laennec and thus advocated the use of the stethoscope in this country.

FORDOUN, John (-d.1384)of Fordoun. Is the chief authority for Scottish history before 1400.

FORRESTER, Charles of Edinburgh. Scientific consultant. Professor of Chemistry, Indian School of Mines (1926), Scientific Officer of the British Coal Utilisation Research Assoc. (1960-63). Held many important posts in India in fuel research.

FORSYTH, Alexander John (1768-1843) of Belhelvie, Aberdeenshire. Inventor and clergyman. In 1807 patented his application of the detonating principle in firearms, which was followed by the adaptation of the percussion cap (1808). He was pensioned by the British Govt. after refusing to sell the secret to Napoleon.

FORSYTH, Andrew (1858-1942) of Glasgow. Mathematician and lecturer. By 1890 was recognised as the most brilliant pure mathematician in the British Empire.

FORSYTH, Ian M. (1892-1969) of Anstruther. UK Delegate to the European Coal Organization (1946-47). Under-Sec. Ministry of Fuel and Power (1946-52).

FORSYTH, William (1737-1804) of Old Meldrum. Gardener who became, in 1784, Superintendent of the Royal Gardens of St James and Kensington. Published several works on diseases, etc. in fruit. The shrub 'Forsythia' bears his name.

FORTUNE, Robert (1813-80) of Berwickshire. Botanist. Travelled extensively in the East, for the London Botanical Society, and introduced many oriental plants into Britain.

FRASER, Alexander (1827-99) Scottish landscape painter.

FRASER, Bill (1908-) of Perth. Comic and Character actor. Played many parts in films and TV. Made his name on TV as 'Snudge' in *The Army Game*. His films incl. *Up Pompeii, Up The Chastity Belt* and *Doctor at Large*.

FRASER, Douglas (1916-) of Glasgow. Elected leader, in 1977, of America's most powerful Union–United Auto Workers.

FRASER, Francis C. (1903-) of Dingwall. Keeper of Zoology, British Museum (Natural History) (1957-). Took part in 'Discovery' investigations (1925-33), and Danish 'Atlantide' expedition, West Africa (1945-46).

FRASER, James Baillie (1783-1856) of Inverness-shire. Traveller, Man of Letters and Explorer. Explored in the Himalayas and travelled extensively in India and Persia.

FRASER, John (1750-1811) of Inverness-shire. Botanist. Introduced many plants to Britain from America and Cuba. Was botanical collecter to the Czar of Russia (1797-98).

FRASER, (John) Malcolm (1930-). His ancestors left Fortrose in early 1800s. Leader of the Australian Liberal Party. Prime Minister of Australia (1975-).

FRASER, Malcolm, (1920-90) of New York, Son of a Scottish tailor. Billionaire publisher. Founder of *Forbes* magazine, the world's leading business magazine. He owned much property in New York.

FRASER, Peter (1884-1950) of Fearn, Ross and Cromarty. Helped to organize the New Zealand Labour Party. Prime Minister of New Zealand (1940-49).

FRASER, (Richard Michael Fraser) of Kilmorack. Life peer (1915-) of Rubislaw, Aberdeen. Director of Glaxo Holdings Ltd. (1975-). Sec. to the Conservative Leaders Consultative Comm. (Shadow Cabinet) (1964-70).

FRASER, Ronald (1930-) of Bonnybridge, Stirlingshire. Actor on stage and screen. Appeared in many films incl. *The Sundowners, The*

*Best of Enemies, The Castaways, Paper Tiger* and many others. His TV films incl. *The Misfit, Mr Big, The Sweeney* and *Spooner's Patch.*

FRASER, Simon (1776-1862). American of Scottish descent. Fur trader and explorer. Explored the Red River and the Fraser River, which is named after him. He was the first to descend the Fraser River to the sea in 1808.

FRASER, Thomas C. (1909-) of Aberdeen. Director Commission on Inquiry into Industrial Relations (1970). Chairman Economic Development Commission for wool textile industry (1971-).

FRASER, Sir Thomas Richard (1841-1920), born in Calcutta of Scottish parents. Pharmacologist. Chairman, Indian Plague Commission (1891-09). President of the Assoc. of Physicians of Gt. Britain and Ireland (1908-09).

FRASER-DARLING, Sir Frank (1903-) of Edinburgh? President, Conservation Foundation, Washington D.C. Hon. Trustee, National Parks of Kenya. Member, Royal Commission on Environmental Pollution (1970-)

FRAZER, Sir James George (1854-1941) of Glasgow. Social Anthropologist, Folklorist, and Classical Scholar. Appointed Professor of Social Anthropology at Liverpool in 1907. His major work is *The Golden Bough* (12 vols.) a study in magic and religion which was published in 1890.

FULTON, Sir John Scott (1902-) of Dundee. Vice-Chancellor of Univ. of Sussex (1959-). Principal, Univ. Coll., Swansea (1947-59), Chairman, Commission on educational requirements of Sierra Leone (1954) and the BBC and ITA Liaison Advisory Committee on Adult Educational Programmes (1962-).

FYFE, Sir William H. (1878-1965) of Edinburgh? Principal and Vice-Chancellor of Queen's Univ., Kingston, Ontario (1930-36) and of the Univ. of Aberdeen (1936-48).

FYFFE, Will (1885-1947) of Dundee. Music hall comedian. Considered one of the best pantomime comedians of his day. One of his most popular songs is 'I Belong to Glasgow'.

# G

GALLOWAY, Sir Alexander (1895-) of Dunbar. High Commissioner and Commander in Chief, British troops, Austria (1947-50). Chairman Jordan Development Bank (1951-52).

GALLOWAY, Sir Archibald (1780-1850) of Perth. Major-General and writer on India.

GALLOWAY, Thomas (1796-1851) of Symington. Mathematician, astronomer and writer.

GALT, John (1779-1839) of Irvine. Novelist. His best works incl. *The Steamboat, The Provost* and *Sir Andrew Wylie* (1822), and *The Entail* (1824). His biographical works included *Life of Byron* (1830). He founded the Canada Company, a commercial enterprise that was disappointing. The town of Galt in Canada is named after him.

GARDEN, Graeme (1943-) of Aberdeen. Actor and scriptwriter. His *I'm Sorry I'll Read That Again* began his TV and showbusiness career. Best known for his part in *The Goodies*.

GEAR, William (1915-) of Methil. Painter. Head of the Faculty of Fine Art and Design, Birmingham (1964-). Has works in permanent collections in many parts of the world.

GED, William (1690-1749) of Edinburgh. Printer and goldsmith. Invented a process of stereotyping in 1725.

GEDDES, Sir Anthony Reay Mackay (1912-), son of Sir Eric Geddes. Chairman of Dunlop Holdings Ltd. (1968-78), President (1978-).

GEDDES, Alexander of Glass near Huntly. Went to America as a young man in the nineteenth century, and later became known as the 'Chicago Grain King'.

GEDDES, Alexander (1737-1802) of Ruthven, Banffshire. Theologian, Bible critic and writer. Made a new translation of the Bible for Catholics (1792-1800). He was also a poet.

GEDDES, Andrew (1783-1844) of Edinburgh. Painter and etcher.

GEDDES, Sir Auckland Campbell, 1st Baron (1879-1954) Surgeon, soldier, professor of anatomy, Cabinet Minister and Ambassador. Sometime Chairman of the Dunlop Rubber Co., and first Chairman Imperial Airways. Co. in 1924. British Ambassador to Washington (1920-24).

GEDDES, Sir Eric (1875-1937), born in Agra, India, of Scottish parents, brother of Sir Auckland. Presided over, what became known as 'The Geddes Axe' committee on National expenditure. Was Director-General of Military Railways (1916-17), and Vice-Admiral and First Lord of the Admiralty (1917). A man of tremendous drive and ability.

GEDDES, Ford Irvine (1913-). Chairman, British Shipping Federation (1965-68), and of P & O Steam Navigation Co. (1971-72).

GEDDES, Jenny, of Edinburgh. A vegetable seller. In 1637, in St Giles she threw a stool at the Dean after the introduction of Land's new prayer book, and shouted, "Thou false thief, dost thou daur say mass at my lug."

GEDDES, Sir Patrick (1854-1932) of Ballater. Botanist, sociologist and pioneer town planner. Has been described as the 'Father of modern town planning', and fifty years ahead of his time. It was he who invented the term 'conurbation'.

GEDDES, Ross Campbell, 2nd Baron, (1907-). Chairman, British Travel Assoc. since 1964. President, Chamber of Shipping of the UK (1968-).

GEDDIE, John Liddell (1881-1969) of Edinburgh. Lecturer d'Anglais at Univ. of Lyons (1903-04) and at Sorbonne, Paris (1905-06). Editor of *Chamber's Journal* (1915-47).

GEIKIE, Sir Archibald (1835-1924) of Edinburgh. Geologist. Was (1882-1901) Director-General of the survey of the UK and head of the Geological Museum, London. President of the Royal Society (1908-13).

GEIKIE, James (1839-1915) of Edinburgh. Geologist brother of Sir Archibald. Wrote a standard work on the Glacial period (1874) and several other geological books.

GEMMELL, Alan Robertson (1913-86) of Troon, Ayrshire. Professor of Biology, Univ. of Keele (1950-). Lecturer and regular broadcaster, since 1950, with the BBC in *Gardeners' Question Time.*

GEORGE, Sir Robert Allingham (1897-1967), son of the late Wm. George of Invergordon. Air Vice-Marshal, Air Attaché, Turkey, Greece and RAF Middle East (1939-44). Governor of Southern Australia (1953-60).

GIBBON, Louis Grassic (1901-35), pen name of James Leslie Mitchell of Aberdeenshire. Novelist famed for his trilogy *Sunset Song* (1932), *Cloud Howe* (1933) and *Grey Granite* (1934).

GIBB, Robert (1845-1932) of Laurieston. Military artist. His *Thin Red Line* brought him international fame in 1881. Curator of the Scottish National Gallery (1895-1907).

GIBBS, James (1682-1754) of Aberdeen. Architect. St Martin-in-the-Fields and Radcliffe Camera Library at Oxford (1737-47) are two of the fine buildings designed by him. His *Book of Architecture* (1728) helped to spread the Palladian style and influenced the design of many churches in America. He was a friend of Wren.

GIBSON, Alexander (1800-67) of Laurencekirk. Botanist. Became, in 1838, Superintendent of the botanical gardens at Dupuri, India, and Conservator of Forests in Bombay (1847-61).

GIBSON, Alexander, of Motherwell. Conductor and Musical Director, Scottish National Orchestra, (1959-). Musical Director, Sadler's Wells Opera (1954-57).

GIFFIN, Sir Robert (1837-1910) of Strathaven. Journalist, economist and statistician. Sometime Comptroller-General of the Commercial Labour and Statistical Dept. of the Board of Trade.

GILCHRIST, Sir Andrew (1910-) of Lesmahagow. Ambassador to the Republic of Ireland (1967), Under-Sec. of State, Commonwealth (1966-67) and Consul-General at Chicago (1960-62). Chairman Highlands and Islands Development Board (1970-76).

GILCHRIST, Rae (1899-) of Edinburgh. Consulting physician and lecturer on disorders of the heart and circulation. Lectured in England, America and Africa.

GILCHRIST, Robert N. (1899-) of Aberdeen. Held many high posts in the Indian Educational Service (1910-37).

GILL, Sir David (1843-1914) of Aberdeen. Astronomer at the Cape Observatory (1879-1907). Pioneered the use of photography as a means of charting the heavens.

GILLESPIE, Dame Helen (1898-) of Edinburgh. Brigadier, Matron-in-Chief and Director of the Army Nursing Services, War Office (1952-56).

GILLIES, John (1747-1846) of Brechin. Historian. Appointed Historiographer Royal for Scotland in 1793. His writings incl. *A History of Greece* (1786) and *A History of the World from Alexander to Augustus* (1807).

GILLIES, Sir William (1898-1973) of Haddington, E. Lothian. Landscape painter. Principal of Edinburgh School of Art (1960-66). Perhaps the best loved of Scottish landscape painters.

GILMOUR, Andrew (1898-) of Burntisland. Shipping Controller, Singapore (1939-41), Defence Intelligence Officer, Hong Kong (1941) and Planning Economist UN Technical Assistance Mission to Cambodia (1953-55).

GLADSTONE, William Ewart of Fasque (1808-98), born in Liverpool of Scots descent. One of the great statesmen of the nineteenth century. He was Prime Minister four times (1868-74), (1880-85), (1886) and (1892-94) during Queen Victoria's reign.

GLAISTER, John (1892-) of Glasgow. Emeritus Professor of Forensic Medicine at the Univ. of Egypt, Cairo, and Medical and Legal Consultant to the Govt. of Egypt (1928-32). External examiner in Forensic Medicine at the Univs. of Edinburgh, Birmingham, Liverpool, Leeds, Aberdeen, St Andrews and Sheffield.

GLEIG, George Robert (1796-1888) of Stirling. Novelist and biographer. Took Orders in 1820 and became Chaplain-General of the Army (1844) and Inspector-General of Military Schools in 1846.

GLEN, Sir Alexander (1912-) of Glasgow. Chairman, British Tourist Auth. (1969-). Leader of Oxford Univ. Arctic Expedition (1935-36). Holder of several British and foreign awards for Anthropology and Geography.

GOODSIR, John (1814-67) of Anstruther. Anatomist best known for his work in Cellular Pathology.

GORDON, Alexander (1669-1751) of Auchintoul. Soldier who was a general in the Russian army for many years.

GORDON, Sir Archibald M. (1892-) of Seaton Lodge. Barrister-at-Law, Counsellor and Labour Attaché, British Embassy, Washington D.C. (1942). President UN League of Lawyers (1956).

GORDON, Charles George (1833-85) descendent of the House of Huntly. Major-General 'Gordon of Khartoum'. Governor of the Sudan (1877-80).

GORDON, Donald (1901-) of Old Meldrum. Chairman and President, Canadian National Railways (1950-). Sometime Director, Trans-Canadian Airlines. Was Deputy Governor, Bank of Canada (1938).

GORDON, Lord George (1750-93). Agitator. Leader of the 'No Popery' riots in London in 1780.

GORDON, Hannah, of Edinburgh. Actress with wide radio and TV experience. Best known for her parts in TV's *My Wife Nextdoor; Dear Octopus; Upstairs, Downstairs* and *Telford's Change.*

GORDON, Harry Alexander Ross (1893-1957) of Aberdeen. Comedian. Made famous by the mythical village of Inversnecky.

GORDON, Hugh W. (1897-) of Dumfries. Professor and consulting physician to Dept. of Skin Diseases, St George's Hosp. Consulting dermatologist to Royal Marsden Hosp. and West London Hospital.

GORDON, Ian A. (1908-) of Edinburgh. Professor of English Language and Literature, Wellington, New Zealand (1936-).

GORDON, Sir James Alexander (1782-1869). Sometime Admiral of the Fleet.

GORDON, Sir John Watson (1790-1864) of Edinburgh. Portrait painter. RA (1851). Appointed Limner to the Queen in Scotland in 1850. Painted many distinguished personages in his time, Sir Walter Scott among them.

GORDON, John Rutherford (1890-1974) of Dundee. Journalist. Editor of the *Sunday Express* (1928-54), Editor-in-Chief (1954-74). Trustee of Beaverbrook Foundation. Gordon introduced the first crossword puzzle to be published in a British newspaper.

GORDON, Noele, London born daughter of an Aberdeen marine engineer. Actress who became famous in the long running TV series *Crossroads.* Winner of the *Sun,* Top TV personality award 1975.

GORDON, Patrick (1635-99) of Aberdeenshire. Soldier of fortune, became a General in the Russian Army in 1688.

GORDON, Percival H. (1884-) of Craigmyle. Judge of Court of Appeal, Saskatchewan (1934-61).

GORDON Sir Robert (1647-1704) of Gordonstoun. Inventor and reputed warlock. Designed a pump for raising water.

GORDON, Thomas, described as 'Father of the Russian Navy'. Made an Admiral by Peter the Great.

GOWDY, Revd John (1869-) of Glasgow. President, Anglo-Chinese College, Foochow (1904-23), Fukien Christian Univ. Foochow (1923-27). Teacher Anglo-Chinese Coll., Foochow (1928-30).

GRAHAM, Fredrick C. Campbell (1908-) of Helensburgh. Major-General, served with distinction (1939-45) in Palestine, North Africa, Crete, Syria, India and Italy. Sometime adviser on recruiting Min. of Defence.

GRAHAM, John Anderson, (1861-) of Dumbartonshire. Philosopher, traveller and missionary to India.

GRAHAM, R.B. Cunningham (1852-1936). Born in London, son of a Scottish laird. Traveller, writer and politician. With Kier Hardie he organized the Scottish Labour Party. Wrote over 30 books on travel and many other stories and biographies. Was elected first president of the Scottish National Party.

GRAHAM, Ronald (1896-1967) of Scottish descent. Air Vice-Marshal. Deputy senior Air Staff Officer, Fighter Command (1939), SASO Flying Training AOA Tech. Training Commands (1940), AOA Bomber Command (1941-42), and Air Officer and Air Chief of Staff HQ Combined Operations (1943). AOC West Africa (1944), Commandant RAF Staff Coll. (1945-46) and of Scottish Police College (1949-57).

GRAHAM, Thomas (1805-69) of Glasgow. Chemist. Became first president of the Chemical Society of London. Sometime Master of the Mint. Developed 'Graham's Law' of the diffusion rates of gases. Known as father of Colloid Chemistry.

GRAHAME, Kenneth (1859-1932) of Edinburgh. Author. Descendent of Robert the Bruce. Secretary to the Bank of England (1898-1907). Wrote books for children including *The Wind in the Willows* (1908). The play *Toad of Toad Hall* (1930) was based on Grahame's book.

GRANT, Alexander L. (1901-) of Aviemore. Appointed Director of Barclay's Bank Ltd. in 1945.

GRANT, Sir Andrew (1890-1967) of Edinburgh. Air Marshal (1946). Director-General, RAF Medical Services, Air Ministry (1946-48).

GRANT, Anne (1755-1838) of Glasgow. Poetess and essaysist. Her *Letters from the Mountains* was a great success.

GRANT, Duncan James C. (1885-) of Rothiemurchus. Painter and designer of textiles and pottery. His painting *Girl at the Piano* is in the Tate Gallery, London.

GRANT, Sir Francis (1803-78) of Perthshire. Has been described as the leading portrait painter of his day.

GRANT, George Munro (1835-1902). Canadian of Scottish descent. Scholar and writer. *Ocean to Ocean* was his most famous book (1873).

GRANT, James Augustus (1827-92) of Nairn. Traveller, explorer and writer. Was an associate of Capt. Speke on expeditions in Central Africa.

GRANT, Sir James H. (1808-75) of Kilgraston. Soldier and General in the British Army. Distinguished himself in the two Sikh wars and the Indian Mutiny.

GRANT, Sir James M. (1903-) of Edinburgh? Lord Lyon King of Arms (1969-). Sec. to the Order of the Thistle (1971-). Writer to the Signet.

GRANT, James Macpherson (1822-85) of Alvie, Inverness-shire. Australian statesman. One of the most prominent land reformers in Australia in his day.

GRANT, John Peter (1807-93). Sometime Indian and Colonial Governor.

GRANT, John S. (1909-) of Inverness-shire. Chief Medical Officer, Brit. Railways Board (1965-). Medical Consultant, National Freight Corp.

GRANT, Neil F. (1882-1968) of Forres. London editor of the *Cape Times, Natal Mercury, Rand Daily Mail* and *Sunday Times of Johannesburg.*

GRANT, Sir Patrick (1804-95) of Auchterblair. Soldier who became a Field-Marshal in 1883.

GRANT, Robert (1814-92) of Granton-on-Spey. Astronomer.

GRANT, Sir Robert McVitie (1894-1947) of Edinburgh. Sometime Chairman of McVitie and Price Ltd.

GRANT, Sir Thomas Dundas (1854-1944) of Edinburgh. Consulting Aurist and Laryngologist, London.

GRAY, Sir Alexander (1882-) of Angus. Professor Emeritus of Political Economy, Univ. of Edinburgh, (1956-). Sat as chairman and member of Govt. Commissions, Committees, Courts of Enquiry, Advisory Councils, etc.

GRAY, James (1877-1969) of Edinburgh. Director, Union Castle Mail Steamship Co. Ltd. (1950-55). Was Chief Superintending Engr., Canadian Pacific Steamships (1913-15). General Manager, and later, Director of Harland and Wolff's Works, London, Liverpool and Southampton (1925-35).

GREEN, Charles E. (1866-1920) of Edinburgh. Publisher. Founded the *Juridical Review* (1887), *Scots Law Times* (1891), *Green's Encyclopaedia* (14 vols. 1895) and many important works on agriculture.

GREGORY, David (1661-1708) of Kinairdy, Perthshire. Mathematician. In 1691 became Savilian Professor of Astronomy at Oxford. He first suggested an achromatic combination of lenses.

GREGORY, Sir David (1909-) of Perthshire. Admiral Supt., HM Dockyard, Devonport (1960-64). Flag officer, Scotland and N. Ireland (1964-66).

GREGORY, James (1638-75) of Drumoak, Aberdeenshire. Mathematician and Astronomer. A leading contributor to the discovery of the differential and integral calculus. Invented the reflector telescope.

GREGORY, James (1753-1821) of Aberdeen. Physician who gave his name to 'Gregorie's Mixture'.

GREIG, Alexis Samuilovich (1775-1848), son of Sir Samuel Greig. Became an Admiral in the Russian Navy and distinguished himself in the Russo-Turkish wars (1807 and 1828-29).

GREIG, Sir Samuel (1735-88) of Inverkeithing. Admiral and Commander in Chief in the Russian Navy. Fought against the Turks (1770) and Swedes (1788). Was known as 'Father of the Russian Navy'. When Greig died Catherine the Great said to Prince Potemkin, "A light has been dowsed—a light which will not be relit whilst you and I are alive."

GRIERSON, Sir Herbert J.C. (1866-1960) of Lerwick. Critic and editor. Edited the poems of Donne (1912). His studies included *Cross Currents in the Literature of the Seventeenth Century* (1929) and *Milton and Wordsworth* (1937).

GRIERSON, Sir James M. (1859-1914) of Glasgow. Lieut.-General. Served with distinction at the battles of Kassassin and Tel-el-Kebir.

GRIERSON, John (1898-1972) of Kilmarnock. British Film Producer. General Manager Canadian Wartime Information Bd. (1942-43), Director, Mass communications UNESCO (1946-48). His productions incl. *Song of Ceylon* (1934), *Night Mail* (1936), *World in Action* series (1942-43) and *This Wonderful World* (TV 1961). He was the creator of documentary films.

GRIEVE, Christopher Murray (1892-1978) of Langholm. Wrote under the pseudonym 'Hugh McDiarmid'. Author, poet and journalist. Prolific writer on political and general matters. His poems incl. 'Three Hymns of Lenin', 'A Kist of Whistles', 'The Battle Continues'. Was a founder member of the Scottish Nationalist Party.

GRIEVE, John (1924-) of Glasgow. Character actor. His most popular TV parts incl. *Oh Brother*, *Vital Spark* and *Doctor at Sea*.

GRIEVE, Sir Robert (1910-) of Glasgow. First Chairman of the Highlands and Islands Development Bd. Prof. of Town and Country Planning at Glasgow Univ. Regarded as one of the top planners of Europe.

GRIEVE, Thomas R. (1909-) of Edinburgh? Chairman and Managing Director, Shell Mex & BP (1965-), and of UK Pipelines Ltd. (1965-).

GRIMOND, Joseph (Jo) Lord Grimond of Firth (1913-) of St Andrews. Barrister and politician. Leader of the Liberal Party (1956-67). Director of Personnel, European office UNWRA (1945-47) etc. Once described as the best Prime Minister Britain never had.

GRUB, George (1812-93) of Aberdeen. Church historian. Was the author of *An Ecclesiastical History of Scotland* (1861).

GUNN, Alexander (1844-1914) of Lybster, Caithness. Surgeon. Assisted Lord Lister in his researches into the use of antiseptics.

GUNN, Sir James (1893-1965). Portrait painter. Best known for his portraits of King George VI, G.K.Chesterton, Hilair Belloc and other celebrities. Became President of the Royal Society of Portrait Painters.

GUNN, John C. (1916-) of Glasgow. Cargill Professor of Natural Philosophy. Lecturer on applied mathematics, Univ. of Manchester (1945-46) and Univ. Coll., London (1946-49).

GUNN, Neil Millar (1891-1973) of Dunbeath, Caithness. Novelist. His best known books incl. *Grey Coast, Morning Tide* (1931), *Butcher's Broom*, (1934), *Highland River* (1937), *The Drinking Well*, (1947) and *Silver Darlings* (1951).

GUTHRIE, Sir Giles (1916-) of Wigtownshire. Merchant Banker. Chairman, Air Transport Insurance, Lausanne, Switzerland. Directorships in several Companies incl. Prudential Assurance Ltd., and Radio Rentals Ltd.

GUTHRIE, Sir James (1859-1930) of Greenock. Painter. Elected RSA (1892) and PRSA (1902-19).

GUTHRIE, Thomas (1803-73) of Brechin. Divine and philanthropist. In eleven months (1845-46) he raised £116,000 for providing Free Church Manses. He used his singular gifts of oratory in the causes of temperance and other social reforms, and in favour of compulsory education.

# H

HADDOW, Sir Alexander (1907-) of Broxburn. Appointed Professor of Experimental Pathology, Univ. of London in 1946. Director of Beatty Research Institute, Cancer Research, Royal Cancer Hosp., Fulham Rd. (1946-69).

HADDOW, Alexander J. (1912-) of Glasgow? Entomologist on Yellow Fever research (1942-45). Epidemologist on East African virus research (1950-52).

HAIG, Douglas, Viscount Dawick and 20th Laird of Bemersyde (1861-1928) of Edinburgh. Field Marshal and Commander in Chief, British Forces in the Great War (1914-18).

HALDANE, Elizabeth Sanderson (1862-1937) of Edinburgh. Author. Wrote *A Life of Descartes* (1905). Translated Hagel and wrote commentaries on George Eliot (1927). She was the first woman JP in Scotland.

HALDANE, James Alexander (1768-1851) of Dundee. Preacher who founded in Edinburgh in 1799 the first Congregational Church in Scotland.

HALDANE, John Scott (1860-1936) of Edinburgh? Eminent physiologist and authority on respiration and the effects of high and low atmospheric pressures in the organism. Studied the effects of industrial occupations upon physiology. Was a director of a mining research lab. in Birmingham. Elected Fellow of New College, Oxford.

HALDANE, Richard Burdon, 1st Viscount Haldane of Cloan (1856-1928) of Edinburgh. Statesman and philosopher. Sec. of State for War (1905-12). His great work was the creation of an expeditionary force, the substitution of the territorial force for the old volunteer and militia and the founding of a general staff.

HALL, Basil (1788-1844) of Edinburgh. Travel writer. His works, *Korea* (1818), *Chile, Peru* and *Mexico* (1824), and his *Travels in North Africa* (1829) were highly popular.

HALL, Sir James (1761-1832) of Dunglass. Geologist. Sought to prove the geological theories of his friend and master (Hutton) in the laboratory, and so founded Experimental Geology.

HALLIDAY, Sir Andrew (1781-1839) of Dumfries. Physician. Inspector of Hospitals in West Indies (1833). Sometime physician to the Duke of Clarence.

HAMILTON, Alexander (1757-1804), born in Leeward Islands of Scottish descent. Statesman. Private Sec. to Washington in the American War of Independence. Elected to the New York Legislature in 1787. Sec. to the Treasury (1789-95). Was killed in a duel with a political opponent.

HAMILTON, David (1768-1843) of Falkirk. Architect. His greatest work was the Palace for the Duke of Hamilton, in Lanarkshire.

HAMILTON, Douglas Douglas–(14th Duke) (1903-1973). Chief pilot, Mount Everest Flight Expedition (1933). Sometime President, Air League of the British Empire. Was Premier Duke of Scotland.

HAMILTON, Gavin (1723-98) of Lanark. Painter and antiquary. His collection of marbles is in the Louvre. His paintings were mainly large historical works.

HAMILTON, Hamish (1900-) of Glasgow. Managing Director, Hamish Hamilton Ltd., publishers since 1931. Was seconded to the US Div. of Min. of Information (1941-45).

HAMILTON, Iain Ellis (1922-) of Glasgow. Composer and pianist. Became Professor of Music at Duke Univ., North Carolina, USA in 1962. Hamilton has composed two symphonies and several operas. His works have attracted universal interest and won the Royal Philharmonic Society prize for his Clarinet Concerto.

HAMILTON, Ian of Paisley ? Author, journalist and drama critic. Editorial Director, The Hutchison Group of Publishing Cos. (1958-62). Editor, *The Spectator* (1962-63) and Chairman, New Drama Group.

HAMILTON, James (-d. 1540) of Ayrshire. Architect of exceptional ability in his day.

HAMILTON, Tarrick (1781-1876). Linguist and orientalist. Translator (1820) of the first four volumes of *Sirat Anterah* (narrative of the poet Antar). Became Sec. of the British Embassy, Constantinople.

HAMILTON, William (1704-54) of Bangour, Linlithgowshire. Poet.

Was the first to translate Homer into blank verse. Best remembered for his ballad 'The Braes of Yarrow'.

HAMILTON, Sir William (1730-1803). Scottish diplomat and antiquarian. Took many observations of volcanic activity and of earthquakes. Wrote an account of Pompeii for the Society of Antiquaries of London. He was one of the owners of the Portland Vase. He married Emma Lyon (1791) who became Nelson's mistress about 1798.

HAMILTON, Sir William (1788-1856) of Glasgow. Philosopher. He invented the doctrine of the quantification of the predicate (a form of syllogism in which both subject and predicate are quantified). He urged that the philosophy of common sense is the highest kind of human speculation and reasoning.

HAMILTON, William R.D. (1895-1969) of Campbeltown. Major-General (1953). Consulting physician MELF (1948-50). Director of Medicine and Consulting Physician to the Army (1951-55).

HAMILTON, Sir William Rowan (1805-65). Born in Dublin of a Scottish family that had settled there. Mathematician. At the age of 22 he was appointed Professor of Mathematics at Trinity Coll., Dublin and Royal Astronomer of Ireland. He invented the terms 'vector' and 'scalar' and was first to represent complex numbers as ordered pairs of real numbers.

HAMILTON, William (c.1665-1751) of Ladyland, Ayrshire. Poet famous for his edition of Blind Harry's 'Wallace' (1722) which inspired Burns.

HAMMERTON, Sir John Alexander (1871-1949) of Alexandria, Dumbartonshire. Journalist and editor. Edited many works of reference incl. the *Universal Encyclopaedia, Universal History, Peoples of all Nations* and *Countries of the World*. In both World Wars he edited a weekly magazine *War Illustrated*.

HANNAY, James (1827-73) of Dumfries. Writer. His best novels were *Singleton Fontenoy* (1850) and *Eustace Conyers* (1855). He was British Consul at Barcelona from 1868 until his death.

HARDIE, James Keir (1856-1915) of Legbrannock, Lanarkshire. Founder of the Independent Labour Party in 1893. In 1906 became first chairman of the Parliamentary Labour Party.

HARDIE, Thomas (1752-1832) of Larbert. Politician. In 1792 he founded the London Corresponding Society for Parliamentary and Social Reform.

HARRISON, James, a Scottish printer emigrant to Australia in 1837. While cleaning type with ether, he noticed its cooling effect on metal – ether being a liquid with a low boiling point that vaporises easily. In 1851 he put his discovery to use by pumping ether through pipes to cool a brewery building in the gold rush town of Bendigo, Victoria. He later developed the first vapour-compressor machines which were produced for several decades, using ethyl ether as the refrigerant. It was Harrison's idea that led to the first successful voyage from Australia with a refrigeration plant in the ss *Strathleven* with a cargo of meat to London in 1880.

HARVEY, Sir George (1805-76) of St Niniane, nr. Stirling. Historical and landscape painter. Appointed President of the Royal Scottish Academy in 1864.

HASTON, Dougal (1939-77) of Currie, Midlothian. First British climber to conquer Mt Everest (1975). Was also the first Briton to climb the north face of the Eiger (1966). Sometime described as the greatest mountain climber ever.

HAY, Ian, Major-General John Hay Beith, (1876-1952) of Edinburgh ? Novelist and dramatist. *The First Hundred Thousand* (1915) and *Carrying On* (1917) were popular books of his. He was Director of Public Relations at the War Office (1938-41).

HAY, Sir Robert (1889-) Lieut.-General and Director-General, Imperial Medical Service and Hon. Physician to the King (1944-48).

HEATHFIELD, George Augustus Eliott, Baron Heathfield, (1717-90) of Stobbs, Roxburghshire. General who served in the war of Austrian Succession at Dettingen and Fontenoy, and in the West Indies in the Seven Years War. As Governor of Gibraltar he defended it against Spanish attacks from 1779 to 1783.

HENDERSON, Arthur (1863-1935) of Glasgow. Labour politician. Home Sec. (1924), Foreign Sec. (1929-31). Was a crusader for general disarmament.

HENDERSON, Sir David (1862-1921) of Glasgow. Lieut.-General. Served with distinction in Sudan and South Africa. Took up flying in 1911 and played a part in the formation of the Royal Flying Corps in 1912.

HENDERSON, David W. (1903-) of Glasgow. Director of Microbiological Research Establishment, Min. of Defence (1946-).

HENDERSON, Frank Young (1894-1966) of Glasgow. Director, Forest Products Research Laboratory, Dept. of Scientific and Industrial Research (1945-60).

HENDERSON, James E. (1923-) of Glasgow. Chief Scientist RAF and member of the Air Force Board (1969-).

HENDERSON, Sir James T. (1901-) of Moffat. Diplomat. Chargé d'Affaires Helsinki (1932-35), Consul General, Houston (1949), Minister for Ireland (1953-56) and Ambassador to Bolivia (1956-60).

HENDERSON, Dame Joan, of Stonehaven. Director, Women's Royal Army Corps (1964-67).

HENDERSON, Joe ('Mr Piano') (?-d. 1980) of Glasgow. Pianist, accompanist and composer of considerable merit.

HENDERSON, Patrick Howart (1876-1968) of Perthsire. Major-General (1931), served with the 7th Div. in France (1914-15), with 28th Div. in Egypt and Macedonia (1916-17) and with 27th Div. in Macedonia, S. Russia and Trans-Caspio (1917-19).

HENDERSON, Peter, of Inverness. Senior Principal Medical Officer, Min. of Education (1964-69).

HENDERSON, Ralph (1897-) of Perth. Director of Stores, Admiralty (1955-60).

HENDERSON, Thomas (1798-1844) of Dundee. Astronomer. In 1831 was appointed Director of the Royal Observatory at the Cape of Good Hope.

HENDRY, Arnold W. (1921-) of Buckie. Professor of Civil Engineering, Univ. of Edinburgh (1964-), Univ. of Khartoum (1951-57). Prof. of Building Science, Univ. of Liverpool (1957-63).

HENDRY, Stephen (1968-) of Edinburgh. Became world champion snooker player in 1990, the youngest ever. An all-time great at the snooker table.

HENRY, Joseph (1797-1878), born in America of Scottish parentage. Physicist. Made important discoveries on the subject of electromagnetic induction; the 'Henry' (of inductance) is named after him. In 1840 he became the first Sec. and Director of Smithsonian Institute, Washington.

HENRY, Robert (1718-90) from near Stirling. Historian. Wrote the *History of Great Britain on a New Plan* (1771-90) in 6 vols.

HERIOT, George (1563-1624) of Edinburgh. Goldsmith, Jeweller and philanthropist, known as 'Jingling Geordie'. Jeweller to James VI and goldsmith to Queen Anne of Denmark (1597). He amassed considerable wealth as a court jeweller in London. Founder of George Heriot's School, Edinburgh.

HERRIES, John Maxwell, 4th Baronet (c.1512-83). Soldier and

politician.Led Mary, Queen of Scots Cavalry at Langside and rode with her into England in 1568.

HERRIOT, James. See WIGHT, J.A.

HETHERINGTON, Sir Hector (1888-1965) of Cowdenbeath. Principal and Vice-Chancellor, Univ. of Glasgow (1936-61). Professor of Logic and Philosophy, Univ. Coll., Cardiff (1915-20), Exeter (1920-24) and Liverpool (1927-36).

HIELBRON, Sir James Morris (1886-1959) of Glasgow. Organic chemist. Professor of Organic Chemistry at Liverpool (1920), Manchester (1933) and at Imperial Coll., London (1938-49). Was best known for his work on vitamins A and D. Elected FRS in 1931.

HIGHET, Gilbert (1906-) of Glasgow. Scholar, critic and author. Appointed Professor of Greek and Latin in Columbia Univ. in 1938. Wrote *Man's Unconquered Mind.*

HILL, David Octavius (1802-70) of Perth. Landscape and portrait painter and photographer. The first to apply photography to portraiture.

HILL, Ian G. W. (1904-) of Edinburgh. Professor of Medicine, Univ. of St Andrews (1950-). Consulting physician, 14th Army, Burma and ALFSEA (1944-45). Patel lecturer, Bombay (1961).

HOARE, Sir Samuel (1896-) of Inverness. Politician. Asst. Under-Sec. of State, Home Office (1946-61). Represented the UK on various international bodies, incl. Narcotics Commission and Economic and Social Council of the UN.

HOGG, James, (1770-1835) of Ettrick, Selkirkshire. Poet of force and originality. 'The Queen's Wake' (1813) was one of his best. He was more commonly known as the 'Ettrick Shepherd'.

HOLDEN, Sir Isaac (1807-97) of Hurlet, Renfrewshire. Inventor and mathematician. Studied chemistry in his leisure hours. Invented the 'Lucifer' match, but was anticipated in this by John Walker of Stockton. Was an associate of Lister.

HOLMES, William (1922-) of Kilbarchan, Renfrewshire. Professor of Agriculture, Wye Coll., London (1955-). President, British Soc. of Animal Production (1969-70). Sometime adviser to the Tech. Committee, Univ. of West Indies.

HOME, John (1722-1808) of Leith. Dramatist and playwright. His first drama *Douglas*, produced at Covent Garden in 1757 was his greatest success.

HONEYMAN, Alexander M. (1907-) of Fife? Professor of Oriental

Languages,Univ. of St Andrews (1936-). External examiner to Univs. of Glasgow, Edinburgh, Belfast, Leeds and London. Travelled and excavated in S. Arabia (1950-54 and 58).

HONEYMAN, Sir George (1898-) of Glasgow. Chairman, Civil Service Arbitration Tribunal (1952), Agricultural Wages Bd. (1953), Comm. of Inquiry, Copper Mining Industry, N. Rhodesia (1957), Bd. of Inquiry, Sugar Milling Industry, Fiji (1959) etc.

HOOD, Sir Alexander (1888-) of Edinburgh. Lieut.-General (1941). Sometime Deputy Director of Medical Services, British Forces in Palestine and Transjordan. Director-General Army Medical Services (1941-48). Governor and C in C, Bermuda (1949-55).

HOOD, Thomas (1799-1845), born in London of Scottish descent. Poet and contributer to the *London Magazine*. Published *Whims and Oddities* (1826) and his *Comic Annual* four years later.

HOPE, John A. Louis, 7th Earl and 1st Marquis of Linlithgow, (1860-1908). Appointed first Governor-General of Australia (1900-02).

HOPE, Thomas Charles (1766-1844) of Edinburgh. Chemist and lecturer. Carried out important researches in physics. Conclusively confirmed the seventeenth century observation—in his day regarded with scepticism—that water expands as it freezes.

HOPE, Victor Alexander John, 8th Earl and 2nd. Marquis of Linlithgow, (1887-1952). Viceroy of India (1936-43).

HORNE, Henry Sinclair, 1st Baron of Stirkoke (1861-1928). Commanded 1st Army in France (1916). General Officer C in C, Eastern Command (1919-23). Was the first to use the 'Creeping Barrage' system of artillary support for infantry.

HORROCKS, William. The Scotsman who invented the first effective mechanical weaving looms in 1803 and 1813. They included automatic unwinding of the warp threads and the winding up of the fabric on the beam.

HORSBURGH, Thomas. Scottish blacksmith. Devised the first steel shafted golf club in 1894.

HOUSTON, Renée (Katherina Houston Gribbin) (-d.1980). Vaudeville and review artist. Once teamed with her sister Billie. More recently, character artist on Screen and TV. Was a popular member of radio's *Petticoat Line* team.

HOUSTON, Sam (1793-1863) US Soldier and Politician of Scottish descent; first President of Texas (1836), Governor of Texas (1859-61). Houston in Texas bears his name.

HOWE, James (1780-1836) of Skirling, Peebles-shire. Artist. His pictures are still much admired. He was commissioned by Sir John Sinclair the noted agriculturist and statesman, to travel Scotland and make paintings of different breeds of cattle.

HOWSON, John, (1908-) of Glasgow. Rear-Admiral (1961). Served with distinction in HMS *Newcastle* and HMS *Nelson* (1939-44). Chief of Staff to C in C Plymouth (1958-61). Commander, Allied Naval Forces, Northern Europe (1961-62). Regional Officer, N. Midlands British Productivity Council (1964-).

HOYER-MILLAR, Dame Elizabeth of Angus. Director, Women's Royal Naval Service (1958-61). Hon. ADC to the Queen (1958-61).

HUGHES, Henry H. (1911-) of Glasgow. Rear-Admiral (1964). Director of Naval Electrical Engineering (1964-).

HUME, Alexr. (c.1560-1609) of Polworth, Berwickshire. Poet and minister. His best known poem 'The Day Estivall'.

HUME, David (1711-76) of Edinburgh. Philosopher, historian and economist. Wrote a *Treatise on Human Nature* (1739-40) and *The History of England* (1754-73).

HUME, Joseph (1777-1855) of Montrose. Radical politician. Sat in Parliament (1812 and 1819-55). Advocated savings banks, freedom of trade with India, abolition of flogging in the army, of naval impressment and of imprisonment for debt, and the repeal of the act prohibiting export of machinery, and of that preventing workmen from going abroad.

HUMPHREY, Sir Andrew (1921-77) of Edinburgh. Marshal of the Royal Air Force. Chief of Air Staff (1974-76) and Chief of the Defence Staff (1976-77).

HUMPHREYS, Eliza M. (-d.1938) from Inverness-shire. Novelist who wrote under the pen-name 'Rita'. Of some 60 novels, *Souls* (1903) was the one that made her famous. In the days of Victorian conventions, she was considered a daring novelist.

HUNT, Sir Peter M. (1916-) of Perthshire. General. Chief of the General Staff (1973-). Was Chief of Staff Scottish Commd. (1962-64). Commander Northern Army Group and C in C BAOR (1970-73).

HUNTER, Sir Archibald. Scottish General in the Sudan with Kitchener.

HUNTER, John (1728-93) of Long Calderwood, E. Kilbride. Physiologist and Surgeon. Founder of Surgical Pathology. His *Natural History of Human Teeth* (1771-78) revolutionised dentistry. In 1776 he was appointed surgeon extraordinary to the King. He was regarded as one of the greatest surgeons of all time.

HUNTER, William (1718-93) of Long Calderwood, and brother of John. Anatomist and obstetrician. He was the leading obstetrician of his time. His chief work was on the uterus. It was he who built the famous Anatomical School in Gt. Windmill St., Leicester Sq. In 1764 was appointed physician extraordinary to Queen Charlotte. Elected FRS in 1767.

HUNTER, Sir William Wilson (1840-1900) of Glasgow. Statistician. Director-General of the Statistical Dept. of India (1871). The Indian census of 1872 was his work.

HUTCHINSON, John (1832-1910) of Edinburgh. Sculptor. His principal works are statues of Robert Bruce, John Knox, Queen Victoria and the Prince Consort.

HUTCHISON, Sir Balfour Oliphant (1889-1967) of Kirkcaldy. Lieut.-General. Deputy QMG Middle East (1940-42), GOC Sudan and Eritrea (1942-43), QMG India (1944-45) (Ret.) Served with distinction in the Palestine Rebellion (1938-39).

HUTCHISON, James H., (1912-) of Glasgow. Samson Gemmel Professor of Child Health. Produced many publications on paediatric problems, rickets and genetic diseases in childhood.

HUTCHISON, Sir William Oliphant (1889-1970) of Fife. Portrait painter. President, Royal Society of Portrait Painters (1965). His sitters included HM The Queen and HRH Prince Philip, Duke of Edinburgh.

HUTCHISON, Dr William W. of Aberdeen. Appointed President of the Geographical Assoc. of Canada in 1973.

HUTTON, James (1726-97) of Edinburgh. Geologist. The 'Huttonian' theory, emphasizing the igneous origin of many rocks and deprecating the assumption of other causes than those we see still at work, was expounded before the Royal Society of Edinburgh in 'A Theory of the Earth' (1785). It formed the basis of modern geology.

# I

IMRIE, Sir John D. (1891-) of Kinross ? Educ. Edinburgh. Chartered Accountant. Local Govt. Commissioner, West Indies (1951-53).

INCHCAPE, (Kenneth J. W. Mackay) 3rd Earl, (1917-). Director, P & O Steam Nav. Co., The Chartered Bank, Royal Exch. Assurance, Burma Oil Co., B.P. Oil Co., Commonwealth Development Finance Co., etc. Appointed Chairman P & O in 1973.

INNES, Cosmo (1798-1874) of Deeside. Antiquary, historian and editor. Author of *Scotland in the Middle Ages* (1860) and *Sketches of Early Scottish History* (1861).

INNES, Lewis (1651-1738) of Banffshire. Became Principal of the Scots College, Paris.

INNES, Thomas (1662-1744) of Aboyne, Aberdeenshire. Historian and antiquary. Became Vice-Principal of Scots Coll., Paris. Wrote *Critical Essay on the Ancient Inhabitants of the Northern Parts of Britain* (1729).

INNES, Sir Thomas of Learney, (1893-). Lord Lyon King of Arms and Sec. to the Order of the Thistle (1946-69). Published many articles on Scots Heraldry, history and peerage law.

INVERCLYDE, Sir John Burns, 1st Baron (1829-1901) of Glasgow. One time chairman of the Cunard Steamship Co.

INVERCLYDE, Sir George A. Burns, 2nd Baron (1861-1905) of Glasgow. Followed his brother John as Chairman of the Cunard Steamship Co.

INVERFORTH, Sir Andrew Weir, 1st Baron (1865-1955). Shipowner. Surveyor-General, Supply, War Office, and member of the War Council (1917-19).

INVERFORTH, Sir Andrew A. M. Weir, 2nd Baron, (1897-). Chairman and Managing Director of Andrew Weir & Co. Ltd.

IRVINE, James Colquhoun (1877-1952) of Glasgow. Chemist. Became famous for his researches in carbohydrate chemistry.

IRVING, David (1778-1860) of Langholm. Biographer, librarian and editor. In 1820 was appointed Principal Librarian of the Faculty of Advocates.

IRVING, David B. (1903-) of Ayrshire. Chairman, London Electricity Board (1956-58), British Electricity Development Assoc. (1960-61) and Power Division IEE (1962-63).

IRVING, Edward (1792-1834) of Annan, Dumfriesshire. From 1822 till his death he was one of the most notable preachers in London (Scotch Church in Hatton Garden and a new church in Regent Sq.). A man of striking appearance and fine voice.

IRVING, John (1920-) of Hamilton? Professor of Natural Philosophy. Senior lecturer in applied mathematics, Univ. of Southampton (1951-59). Prof. and Head of Dept. of Applied Mathematics and Theoretical Physics, Univ. of Cape Town (1959-61).

IRVING, Washington (1783-1859), born in New York, son of a Scottish emigrant. Essayist and historian. *The Sketch Book* (1819) which contained 'Rip Van Winkle' and 'The Legend of Sleepy Hollow' was a great success. His crowning work was the *Life of Washington* (1855-59).

ISAACS, Alick (1921-67) of Glasgow. Virologist and discoverer of Interferon in 1952.

IVORY, James (1765-1842). A brilliant Scottish mathematician who won considerable fame in his day.

# J

JACK, Sir Daniel (1901-) of Glasgow. Professor of Economics, Univ. of Durham and King's Coll., Newcastle upon Tyne (1950-55). Chairman, Court of Inquiry, Shipping and Engineering wages dispute (1957), London Airport dispute (1958) and Ford dispute (1963). Appointed Chairman, Air Transport Board in 1961.

JACK, Gilbert (c.1578-1628) of Aberdeen. Metaphysician and medical writer. Was first to teach metaphysics at Leyden. Declined a professorship at Oxford in 1621.

JACK, Robert L. (1845-) of Irvine. Consulting geologist, mining engineer and explorer in Queensland. Was Govt. Geologist for Queensland (1877-99).

JACK, William (1795-1822) of Aberdeen. Botanist and surgeon. Appointed surgeon in Bengal Medical Service when aged 18.

JACK, William (1834-1924) of Stewarton. Astronomer and philosopher. Prof. of Astronomy, Univ. of Glasgow and Prof. of Natural Philosophy, Manchester (1866-70).

JACKSON, Gordon, (1923-90) of Glasgow. Popular actor with wide experience in films and TV. His some 60 films incl. *The Captive Heart* (1946), *Whisky Galore* (1948), *The Lady with a Lamp* (1951), *Tunes of Glory* (1960) and *Cast a Giant Shadow* (1966). Famous for his part as Hudson in TVs *Upstairs Downstairs* (1972-85) and his leading part in the TV series *The Professionals*.

JACOB, Violet Kennedy-Erskine (1863-1946) of Dun, Montrose. Poetess and novelist. Her poems incl. 'The Northern Lights' (1927), and two of her best known novels are *The Interloper* (1904) and *Flemington* (1911).

JAMESON, George (1588-1644) of Aberdeen. Portrait painter, sometimes called 'the Scottish Van Dyke'.

JAMESON, Sir Leander Starr (1853-1917) of Edinburgh. Politician and administrator in South Africa. In 1893 Jameson took a leading part in a war which ended in the capture of Matabeleland.

JARDINE, James (1928-) from near Hawick. Policeman who became chairman of the Police Federation of England and Wales (1976-82).

JARDINE-PATERSON, Sir John of Lockerbie. President, Bengal Chamber of Commerce and Industry (1966) and Assoc. Chamber of Commerce, India. Member of local board Reserve Bank of India (1965-67) and many other important posts at home and abroad.

JARVIE, John Gibson (1883-1964) of Carluke. Founder and chairman from its beginning in 1919 of United Dominions Trust Ltd., and the UDT group of companies until 1963 when he retired from the Chair and became President.

JEFFREY, Francis, Lord Jeffrey (1773-1850) of Edinburgh. Critic and Judge. Became Lord Advocate in 1830 and entered Parliament.

JEFFREY, John, of Fife. Gardener. Worked in Oregon and California. Discovered the Western Hemlock, and the Jeffrey Pine bears his name.

JEFFREY, William (1896-1946) of Kirk o'Shotts, Lanarkshire. Poet, journalist and dramatic critic.

JOHNSTON, Alexander Keith (1844-79) of Edinburgh. Writer of geographical works. In 1879 was appointed leader of the Royal Geographical Society's expedition to East Africa.

JOHNSTON, Archibald, Lord Warriston (1611-63) of Edinburgh. Advocate and statesman. Raised to the peerage by Cromwell. Appointed Commissioner-Judge of Scotland. After the Restoration he was executed at Edinburgh.

JOHNSTON or Ronston, Arthur (1587-1641) of Aberdeenshire. Physician and humanist. Practised medicine in France whence his fame as a latin poet spread over Europe. About 1625 he was appointed physician to Charles I.

JOHNSTON, Dr James (1854-1921) of Huntly. Physician and evangelist. In 1876 he was the founder of Jamaica Evangelistic Mission.

JOHNSTON, John Lawson, an Edinburgh butcher who invented Bovril. In about 1863 John concocted a drink he called 'fluid beef', which was a great success. He later went to Canada where he developed a concentrated version which he had patented as 'Bovril'.

JOHNSTONE, Alan S. of Dumfriesshire. Professor of Radiodiagnosis, Univ. of Leeds (1948-68). President, Thoracic Society of Gt. Britain (1961-62). Produced several publications on Radiology.

JOHNSTONE, Alexander V. R. (1916-) of Glasgow. Air Vice-Marshal, founder of the Malayan Air Force (1957), Director of Personnel, Air Ministry (1962-64), AOC No. I8 Gp. and Maritime Air Commander, North Atlantic, NATO (1965-68).

JORDAN, Sydney (1929?-) of Dundee. Author and cartoonist. Creator of 'Jeff Hawk' the *Daily Express* cartoon spaceman. Awarded the Prix St Michel by a European Cartoonists Assoc. in 1973.

JUNOR, John (1919-) of Black Isle. Editor, *Sunday Express* (1954-). Became a Director of Beaverbrook Newspapers in 1960. Was Deputy Editor, *Evening Standard* (1953-54).

JUSTICE, James Robertson (1905-75) Scottish actor and personality. Former journalist and naturalist. Starred in many American and British films, incl. *Scott of the Antarctic* (1948), *Whisky Galore* (1949), *Doctor in the House* (1954), *Campbell's Kingdom* (1957) *Doctor at Large* (1958) and *Chitty Chitty Bang Bang* (1968).

# K

KAY, Sir James Reid (1885-1965) of Glasgow. President, Imperial Bank of India (Bengal), (1933-34, 1935-36, and 1939-40). Pres. Associated Chambers of Commerce of India (1937-38).

KAY, Katherine Cameron of Glasgow. Painter and etcher. Exhibited at the Royal Academy, Royal Scottish Academy, Berlin, Liverpool, Venice, Leipzig, etc.

KEILLER, Mrs Keiller of Dundee. Invented marmalade in 1797. Her son founded the Keiller Co., and marmalade became popular throughout the world.

KEIR, Andrew (1926-) of Shotts. Actor. Became popular as Adam Smith the Scottish minister on TV. Played Cromwell in *A Man for all Seasons*, Prince John in TV's *Ivanhoe*. Won an award for his leading part in *Soldier, Soldier*.

KEIR, James (1735-1820) of Edinburgh. Chemist who became a pioneer in industrial chemistry.

KEITH, Sir Arthur (1866-1955) of Old Macher, Aberdeenshire. Anatomist and anthropologist. Wrote *Introduction to the Study of Anthropoid Apes* (1896), *Human Embryology and Morphology* (1901) and works on evolution and the origin of man. Elected FRS.

KEITH, Arthur Berriedale (1879-1944) of Edinburgh. Sanskritist and Constitutional Lawyer. He became a leading authority on constitutional law.

KEITH, George (1685-1778). Close friend of Frederick the Great. He was the last Earl Marshal of Scotland.

KEITH, George (c.1639-1716), Scottish Quaker missionary. Emigrated to Philadelphia in 1689, and was banned from preaching there in 1692.

KEITH, James Francis Edward (1691-1758) of Inverugie, near Peterhead. Soldier who became a Field Marshal and Commander in Chief to Frederick the Great.

KELVIN of Largs, William Thomson, 1st Baron (1824-1907), born in Belfast of Scottish descent. Physicist, mathematician, philosopher and engineer. Discovered the second law of thermodynamics. Inventor of telegraphic and scientific instruments, etc., incl. the improved mariner's compass and sounding equipment. Elected FRS in 1851. Buried in Westminster Abbey.

KEMP, George Meikle (1795-1844) from near Biggar. Draughtsman and Architect. Designer of the Scott Monument, Edinburgh.

KENNEDY, David (?-d.1886) of Perth. Singer who had great success in London, Australia, South Africa, New Zealand, India, Canada and USA.

KENNEDY, James (c.1406-66). Cleric and Statesman. Was Bishop of St Andrews. Took an active part in the politics of Scotland. Acted as Regent during the minority of James III. Was the founder of St Salvators Coll., St Andrews.

KENNEDY, Sir James Shaw (1788-1865) of Kirkcudbrightshire. Soldier. Became a General and distinguished himself under Wellington.

KENNEDY, John (1769-1855) of Kirkcudbrightshire. Cottonspinner and inventor. Introduced several ingenious improvements in the spinning of fine yarns, including the 'Jack Frame'.

KENNEDY, Ludovic (1919-) of Edinburgh. Writer and broadcaster. TV broadcasts incl., ITN newscaster (1956-58), Introduced *This Week* (1958-60), Commentator, *Panorama* (1960-63). Many films incl. *The Singers and the Songs*, *Scapa Flow*, *The Sleeping Ballerina*, *U-boat War*, and *The Rise of the Red Navy*. His books incl. *Sub-lieutenant*, *One Man's Meat*, *The Trial of Stephen Ward*, and *The Life and Death of the Tirpitz*.

KER, William Paton (1855-1923) of Glasgow. Scholar, talker, lecturer and writer. Professor of English at Cardiff (1883), at London (1889) and of Poetry at Oxford (1920). He died of heart failure while climbing in the Alps at the age of 67.

KERR, Deborah Jane (1921-) of Helensburgh. Actress. World famous with many notable successes. Her most powerful performance was perhaps her part in *From Here to Eternity* (1953)

KERR, John (1824-1907) of Ardrossan. Physicist and lecturer in mathematics. In 1876 he discovered the 'magneto-optic effect' which was then named after him. He was the author of *An Elementary Treatise on Rational Mechanics* (1867). Elected FRS.

KENNETH I, called MacAlpine (-d. c.858). Scottish king who conquered the Picts (c.843). He made Dunkeld the ecclesiastical centre of his kingdom. Kenneth invaded England six times.

KIDSON, William (1849-) of Falkirk. Became Prime Minister of Australia in 1906.

KILBRANDON, (Charles J. D. Shaw) Baron (life peer), (1906-) of Kilbrandon, Argyll. Lord of Appeal in Ordinary (1971-). Member, Commission on the Constitution (1969-72), Chairman (1972-73).

KILMARNOCK, (Gilbert A. R. Boyd) 6th Baron (1903-) son of the 21st Earl of Errol. Chairman, Baltic and Mercantile Shipping Exchange (1965-67). He was President, London Chamber of Commerce (1961-63). Freeman of the City of London.

KILMUIR, Viscount, formerly, Sir David P. Maxwell-Fyffe, (1904-). Lawyer and politician. Was Deputy Chief Prosecutor at the Nuremberg Trial of Nazi war criminals.

KINNEAR, Norman Boyd (1882-1957) son of an Edinburgh architect. Was Curator of Bombay Natural History Museum for 12 years, as well as asst. editor of the Bombay Natural History Society Journal. Became keeper of Zoology in the British Museum in 1945, and later Director of the Natural History Dept. there.

KINNEAR, Sir John Macdonald (1782-1830) of Carnden, Linlithgow. Traveller and diplomat. He was Envoy to Persia (1724-30), took part in the hostilities with Russia. He published the results of his numerous journeys in *A Narrative of Travels in Asia Minor, Armenia and Kurdistan* (1813-14).

KINNEAR, Roy (d. 1988) born in Wigan, son of a professional Scots rugby player. Popular actor and comedian. Died following a fall when riding during the making of a film in Spain.

KINNAIRD, Arthur F., 10th Baron (1814-87) of Perthshire. Banker and philanthropist.

KINROSS, (John P. D. Balfour) 3rd Baron of Glasclune (1904-). Author and journalist. Travelled extensively in the Middle East, Africa and elsewhere. Was First Sec. and Director, Publicity Section, British Embassy Cairo (1944-47).

KIRK, James B., (1893-) of Falkirk. Director Medical and Health Dept., Mauritius (1926-41), of Medical Services, Gold Coast (1941-44), of Health Div. Greece Mission UNRRA, (1945-). Chief Medical

Officer, Central HQ Displaced Persons Operations, UNRRA, Germany (1945).

KIRK, Sir John (1832-1922), from near Arbroath. Physician and naturalist. Served as a doctor in the Crimean War, and later he went with Livingstone's second exploring expedition in 1858. Became Consul at Zanzibar in 1873 where he secured the abolition of the slave trade in the dominions of the Sultan of Zanzibar. His name is perpetuated in Nyasaland in the Kirk range, west of Shire River.

KIRKPATRICK, Charles (1879-1955) of Pitlochry. Major-General (1929) in the Indian Army. Served with distinction in the Great War and on the NW Frontier.

KIRKPATRICK, Herbert James (1910-) son of Major-General Charles. Air Vice-Marshal, served on Air Staff, Fighter Command (1939-40), Bomber Commd., (1941-45), and Transport Commd. (1946-48). Chief of Staff 2nd. Allied Tactical Air Force (1957-60) and AOC No.25 Group (1961-63).

KNOX, John (1505-72) of Haddington. Preacher and reformationist. Founder of the Presbyterian Church.

KNOX, John (1913-). Scientist. Appointed Chief Scientific Officer, Min. of Technology in 1965. Head of Research Div., Dept. of Trade and Industry (1971-).

KNOX, Joseph A.C. (1911-) of Aberdeen. Professor of Physiology, University of London at Queen Elizabeth Coll. from 1954.

KNOX, Dr Robert (1791-1862) of Edinburgh. Anatomist and ethnologist. He was the first to bring comparative anatomy to the explanation of human anatomy. Attracted some odium through having obtained subjects for dissection from Burk and Hare.

KYLE, Elizabeth (Agnes M. R. Dunlop) of Ayrshire. Novelist and writer of books for children. Since her first novel in 1932 she published over 50 books.

# L

LAIDLAW, William (1780-1845) of Blackhouse, Selkirk. Poet and general adviser to Sir Walter Scott. He wrote a number of lyrics and ballads.

LAING, Alexander Gordon (1793-1826) of Edinburgh. Explorer of Western Africa. Was sent to explore the source of the Niger River, which he found. Believed to be the first European to have reached the ancient city of Tombouctou (Timbuktu). Was murdered after leaving Timbuktu.

LAING, David (1793-1878) of Edinburgh. Antiquary. From 1837 he was Librarian to the Signet Library.

LAING, Malcolm (1762-1818) of Orkney. Historian. He it was who completed Henry's *History of Great Britain* (1793) and in 1802 published his own *History of Scotland (1603-1701).*

LAING, Ronald David (1927-) of Glasgow. Psychoanalyst. His work involved research into schizophrenia and into the way the family affects the mental states of its individual members.

LAING, Samuel (1780-1868) of Orkney. Traveller and writer in Norway, Sweden, Russia, France, etc.

LAING, W. J. Scott (1914-) of Edinburgh ? One time Chief, Sales Section UN Secretariat. Was Consul, New York (1950) and Consul-General (Commercial), New York (1954).

LAIRD, John, (1805-74) of Greenock. Shipbuilder. One of the earliest constructors of iron vessels.

LAIRD, John, (1887-1946) of Kincardineshire. Philosopher. Professor at Dalhousie, Nova Scotia (1912), Belfast (1913-24) and Aberdeen (1924-26)

LAIRD, Macgregor (1808-61) of Greenock. Explorer, shipbuilder and merchant. Helped to open up the Niger River. Sought to undermine the slave trade in West Africa by promoting legitimate commerce.

LAMOND, Fredric (1868-1948) of Glasgow. Pianist and composer. Made his debut at Berlin in 1885. He excelled in playing Beethoven.

LAMONT, Johann von (1805-79) of Inverey, Braemar. Astronomer. Appointed Director of Bogenhausen Observatory in 1835, and in 1852 became Prof. of Astronomy at Munich.

LANDSBOROUGH, William (1825-) of Stevenston, Ayrshire. Explorer, who with John McDouall Stuart, was first to cross Australia in 1861-62.

LANG, Andrew, (1844-1912) of Selkirk. Scholar and writer of poetry, fiction, fairy tales, folklore and translations from classics. Published *A History of Scotland* (1900-07).

LANG, Cosmo Gordon, Baron Lang of Lambeth (1864-1945) of Fyvie. Anglican Prelate. Archbishop of York (1909-28) and Archbishop of Canterbury (1928-42).

LAPWORTH, Arthur (1892-1941) of Galashiels. Organic chemist. Remembered for his enunciation of the electronic theory of organic clinical reactions in 1920. Appointed to the Chair of Physical and Inorganic Chemistry in 1922. Elected FRS.

LARGE, Eddie (1942-) of Glasgow. Impressionist and comedian. Best known as the duo 'Little and Large' after he teamed up with Syd Little of Manchester.

LAUDER, Sir Harry (Maclennan) (1870-1950) of Portobello. Comedian, singer and composer. 'Roamin in the Gloamin', 'Tobermory', 'A Wee Deoch an' Doris', 'The Lass of Killiecrankie' and 'I Love a Lassie' are some of his best remembered.

LAUDER, Sir Thomas Dick (1784-1848) of Haddington. Novelist and Journalist. Best known for *The Wolf of Badenoch* (1827) and his *Account of the Great Floods in Morayshire* (1829).

LAURIE, John (1897-1980) of Dumfries. Character actor on stage and screen. Popular member of *Dad's Army* series on TV.

LAURIE, Sir John E. (1897-) Major-General. Commanded the 6th Bn. Seaforth Hrs. (1918-19), and 2nd Seaforth Hrs. (1934-38), the Tientsin Area British troops in China (1939-40), No.157 Infantry Bde., France (1940) and 52nd Lowland Div. (1941-42).

LAURIE, Sir Peter (1778-1861) of Haddington. Son of a farmer who became Lord Mayor of London in 1832.

LAW, Andrew Bonar (1858-1923), born in Canada of Scottish descent. Became Prime Minister of Great Britain (1922-23).

LAW, John (1671-1729) of Edinburgh. Financier. Originator of the 'Mississippi scheme'. Having killed a man in a duel, he fled to Holland in 1697, where he studied banking. In 1700 he unsuccessfully proposed a system of paper currency.

LEASK, Sir Henry (1913-). Lieut.-General. GOC Scotland and Governor of Edinburgh Castle (1969-).

LEASK, Kenneth (1896-) of Birsay, Orkney. Air Vice-Marshal. Senior Engineering Staff Officer, HQ RAF India (1933-34) and HQ ADGB Bomber Commd. (1934-40). Director-General Engineering, Air Ministry (1947-49).

LECKIE, Robert, educ. Glasgow. Air Marshal. Director of Flying Ops., Canadian Air Board (1920), Commander (RAF) on HMS *Hermes* and *Courageous* aircraft carriers (1925-29). Director of Training, Air Ministry (1935-38) and Chief of Staff RCAF (1944).

LEE, James Paris (1831-1904) of Hawick. Watchmaker. Invented the remarkably efficient bolt action and magazine of the Lee-Metford (later Lee-Enfield) rifle about 1890.

LEE, Robert (1804-68) of Tweedsmouth. Divine and Reformationist. His introduction of a harmonica (1863) and an organ (1865) and standing during the singing of hymns, brought bitter attacks upon him.

LEGGE, James (1815-97) of Huntly. Missionary and Chinese scholar. Took charge of the Anglo-Chinese College, Malacca (1839-42), then laboured 30 years in Hong Kong. In 1876 he became Professor of Chinese at Oxford. He won a world-wide reputation through his translations of the Chinese classics.

LEISHMAN, Sir William B. (1896-1926) of Glasgow. Bacteriologist. Professor of Pathology in the Army Medical Coll. (1923). He discovered an effective vaccine for innoculation against typhoid, and was first to discover the parasite of the disease kala-azar.

LEITCH, Archibald (1878-1931) of Bute. Physician and bacteriologist. Remembered mainly for his work on cancer research in Middlesex Hosp.

LEITCH, Isabella, of Peterhead. Director, Commonwealth Bureau of Animal Nutrition (1940-60). Produced several publications on genetics, physiology and nutrition.

LEITCH, William Leighton (1804-83) of Glasgow. Watercolour

painter. Was drawing master to Queen Victoria and the Royal Family for 22 years.

LEITH, Sir James (1763-1816) of Aberdeenshire. Lieut.-General. Distinguished himself at Corunna, Busaco, Badajoz and Salamanca.

LENNON, Gordon, (1911-) of Aberdeen. Dean of the Faculty of Medicine, Univ. of Australia, Perth, (1967). Visiting professor to Iraq, Turkey, South Africa and Uganda (1958) and Iran (1959).

LESLIE, Alexander, Lord Belgonie, 1st Earl of Leven (c.1580-1661) of Cupar-Angus. General. Won much distinction in 30 years in the armies of Charles II and Gustavus Adolphus of Sweden. Made Field Marshal of Sweden in 1636. Returned to Scotland in 1638 to serve with the Covenanters. He also distinguished himself at Marston Moor for Charles I.

LESLIE, David, Lord Newark (1601-82) of Fifeshire. General who also served with distinction with Gustavus Adolphus of Sweden. He returned to Scotland about 1643 to aid the Covenanters.

LESLIE or Lesley, John (1527-96), son of the Rector of Kingussie. Was confidential friend of Mary, Queen of Scots, who made him her Ambassador to Queen Elizabeth of England. He became Vicar-General of the diocese of Rouen in 1579.

LESLIE, Sir John (1766-1832) of Largo, Fifeshire. Mathematician, Natural Philosopher and Inventor. Travelled as a tutor in USA and the Continent. Invented a Differential Thermometer, Hygrometer, Photometer, Pyrometer, Atometer and Althriscope. His researches appeared in 1804 in his *Experimental Inquiry into the Nature and Properties of Heat.* In 1810 he successfully applied the absorbent powers of sulphuric acid to freeze water under the receiver of the airpump. This is the first recorded achievement of artificial congelation.

LESLIE, Walter (1606-67). General and diplomat. Served with distinction in Germany against the Swedes.

LEYDEN, Dr John Casper (1775-1811) of Denholm, Roxburghshire. Poet and Orientalist. Studied medicine, was licensed as a preacher in 1798. Went to India (1803) as Asst. Surgeon at Madras. Travelled widely in the East. Acquired 45 languages and translated the Gospels into five of them.

LIDDELL, Eric H. (1902-45) born in China, son of a Scottish missionary. Athlete and missionary to China. Gold medal winner at the 1924 Olympic games in Paris where he created a new quarter mile world record. Became known as the 'Flying Scotsman'.

LIND, James (1716-94) of Edinburgh. Physician. His work towards the cure and prevention of scurvy, induced the Admiralty in 1795 to issue the order that the Navy should be supplied with fresh citrus fruit and lemon juice, and that it should be taken daily. His *A Treatise of Scurvy* (1753) was, and is, a classic of medical literature, and won him an international reputation.

LINDSAY, Alexander Dunlop. 1st Baron Lindsay of Birker (1879-1952) of Glasgow. Scholar and lecturer. In 1949 was appointed head of the new Univ. Coll. of North Staffordshire. Vice-Chancellor of Oxford (1935-38).

LINDSAY, Sir David (sometimes Lyndsay) (1490-1550) of the Mount of Fife. Poet and Lyon King-of-Arms. A favourite of King James V of Scotland. His longest poem 'The Monarchie', giving an account of the rise and fall of Syria, Persia, Greece and Rome, ends with an attack on the Church of Rome.

LINDSAY, Edward S. (1905-) of Fife. Major-General, Controller of Munitions, Min. of Supply (1961). Principal Staff Officer to High Commissioner, Malaya (1954-56)

LINDSAY, James Bowman (1799-1862) of Carmyllie, nr. Arbroath. Teacher, scientist and inventor of the first electric light bulb by carbon filament in a glass tube from which air had been extracted by a vacuum pump (1834-35) some 44 years ahead of Swan and Edison. He never patented his invention and made nothing from it.

LINDSAY, John Mauric (1918-) of Glasgow. Poet and critic. In 1946 he edited the anthology *Modern Scottish Poetry (1920-45)*.

LINTON, Hercules, of Inverbervie. Designer of the famous tea clipper 'Cutty Sark'.

LINKLATER, Eric (1899-1974) of Dounby, Orkney. Novelist and playwright. Was for a time after the Great War, a journalist in Bombay. A prolific writer. His filmed works incl. *Poet's Pub*, *Private Angelo* and *Laxdale Hall*. He was awarded the Carnegie medal for *The Wind on the Moon*. Altogether he published over 70 books, plays and pamphlets.

LIPTON, Sir Thomas Johnstone, (1815-1931) of Glasgow. Businessman and philanthropist. Tea trader, chain store operator and yacht racer.

LISTON, Robert (1794-1847) of Ecclemachin, Linlithgow. Surgeon, whose skill won him reputation in Europe. In 1835 he became Professor of Clinical Surgery at Univ. Coll., London. He was the first to use a general anaesthetic in a public operation (1846). In the pre-anaesthetic era he amputated a patient's leg through the thigh in 33 seconds, and accidentally cut three fingers off his assistant in the process. Liston is said to have been a man of herculean strength.

LITHGOW, William (1582-c.1650) of Lanark. Traveller and writer. In 1612 set out on foot from Paris to Palestine and Egypt. His second tramp (1614-16) led him through North Africa from Tunis to Fez and home via Hungary and Poland. In his last journey (1619-21) to Spain via Ireland he was seized as a spy at Malaga and tortured. He claimed to have tramped 36,000 miles in 19 years.

LIVINGSTONE, David (1813-73) of Blantyre. Explorer and missionary in Africa. Discovered the Zambesi River, Victoria Falls, lakes Nyasa, Shirwa, Mweru, and Bangweulu. Buried in Westminster Abbey.

LOCKHART, John Gibson (1794-1854) of Wishaw, Lanarkshire. Biographer and novelist. His *Life of Sir Walter Scott* (1837-38) is now a classic, and regarded as one of the greatest biographies in the language.

LOCKHART, Sir Robert Hamilton Bruce (1887-1970) of Anstruther, Fife. Author and journalist. Between 1911 and 1917 was British Vice-Consul, then Consul in Moscow. His books incl. *Memoirs of a British Agent, Retreat from Glory, Comes the Reckoning* and *My Europe*.

LOCKHART, William Ewert (1846-1900) of Annan. Subject painter. Painted the Jubilee celebrations in Westminster (1887). Was popular too as a portrait painter. Elected FRS in 1878.

LOGAN, James (Jimmy), (1928-) of Glasgow. Actor/comedian. Appeared in many TV variety shows including his own TV series (1959-61). London Palladium (1969-70).

LOGAN, John (1748-98) of Sontra, Midlothian. Poet and minister. His works included *A Review of the Principal Charges against Warren Hastings* (1788) and *View of Ancient History* (1788-93). His ballad 'Braes of Yarrow' was particularly beautiful.

LOGAN, Sir William Edmund (1798-1875) of Montreal, Canada. Grandson of James Logan of Stirling. Geologist and surveyor. Directed the Canadian Geological Survey (1842-71) and surveyed some 1,000,000 square miles of Lower Canada.

LONGMUIR, Harry (1923-) of Glasgow. Journalist. Voted Journalist of the Year in 1975.

LORIMER, James (1818-90) of Perthshire. Jurist and writer. He was an eminent authority on International Law. *The Institutes of the Law of Nations* was his most important book.

LORIMER, Sir Robert Stodart (1864-1929) of Edinburgh. Architect. His Scottish War Memorial at Edinburgh Castle and the Thistle Chapel in St Giles brought him international recognition.

LOUDON, John Claudius (1783-1843) of Cambuslang. Horticultural writer and landscape gardener. He designed the Birmingham Botanic Gardens in 1828. The cemeteries at Southampton and Bath were also from his designs. His publications inc. *Encyclopaedia of Gardening* (1822), *Encyclopaedia of Agriculture* (1823) and *Encyclopaedia of Plants* (1829).

LOW, Archibald Montgomery (1886-1956). Physicist and inventor, educated at Skerry's Coll., Glasgow. His numerous inventions incl. a system of radio signalling, a television system (1914), electrical rocket control (1917), a coal fuel engine, radio torpedo control gear, the vibrometer and audiometer. Was president of the British Institute of Engineering Technology and of the Institute of Patentees.

LOW, Sir Francis (1893-) of Aberdeenshire. Editor of the *Evening News* of India (1922), News Editor *Times of India* (1925) and Editor (1932-48). President of Bombay YMCA (1943-48).

LOWE, Peter (c.1550-1612). Scottish surgeon. Studied and practised in France. In 1596 he published *A Discourse of the Whole Art of Chyrurgerie*—one of the best works of the period on this subject. He founded the Faculty of Physicians and Surgeons in Glasgow in 1599.

LOVAT, (Simon C. J. Fraser) 17th Baron (1911-). Distinguished himself as a Brigadier in the Commandos in 1943. Under-Sec. of State for Foreign Affairs (1945-).

LUCAS, Raleigh B. (1914-) of Edinburgh. Professor of Oral Pathology, Univ. of London (1954-). Consultant pathologist, Royal Dental Hosp. of London (1950-54).

LULU, (Marie McDonald Mclauchlin Lawrie) of Lennoxtown, Stirlingshire. Actress and singer. Had her own several very successful series with the BBC. Is very popular in America.

LYLE, Alexander (Sandy) (1958-). Golfer with an international reputation.

LYALL, William C. (1921-) of Kelty. Consul-General, Genoa (1969-).

LYELL, Sir Charles (1797-1875) of Kinnordy, near Kirriemuir. Geologist. His *Principals of Geology* (1830-33) may be ranked with

Darwin's *Origin of Species*, among the books which exercised the most powerful influence on scientific thought in the nineteenth century. It denied the necessity of stupendous convulsions, and taught that the greatest geological changes may have been produced by forces still at work. He was buried in Westminster Abbey.

LYNEDOCH, Thomas Graham, 1st Baron (1748-1843) of Balgowan. In 1793 he raised the 99th Reg. of Foot and served at Quiberon and Minorca (1798), besieged Valetta (1800), was at Corruna and Welcheren (1807), defeated the French at Barrosa (1911), Captured Tolosa (1813) and Sabastian, and in Holland conquered at Marxem.

LYNDSAY or Lindsay, Sir David (c.1486-1555) of near Coupar. Poet and artist. Went on Embassies to the Netherlands, France, England and Denmark. His poems, often coarse, are full of humour and knowledge of the world, and were said to have done more for the Reformation in Scotland than all the sermons of Knox.

LYTE, Henry Francis (1793-1847) of Ednam, Roxburghshire. Poet and hymn writer. 'Abide with me' being his best known hymn.

# M

(All names beginning Mc or Mac are treated as if they began Mac.)

MacADAM, Sir Ivison (1894-) of Edinburgh. One-time editor of *The Annual Register of World Events*.

MacADAM, John Loudon (1756-1836) of Ayr. Inventor of the macadamizing system of road making, commonly known as 'Tarmac'. Appointed surveyor of Britain's roads in 1827. He refused a knighthood.

McALISTER, Arthur (1818-) of Glasgow. Became Prime Minister of Australia in 1866.

McALPINE, Sir Robert of Newarthill, near Glasgow. Founder of the Sir Robert McAlpine Construction and Property Empire. Pioneered the widespread use of concrete in Britain.

MacARTHUR, Helen, of Glasgow. Singer. Became popular in radio's *Friday Night is Music Night*. Gained 'Top female radio personality' award in 1971. Had her own TV series *The Helen McArthur Show*.

MacASKILL, Angus (1825-63) of the Isle of Berneray. A 7' 9" giant. Believed to have been the strongest man that ever lived.

MacAULAY, Thomas B. Lord (1800-59). Brilliant Scottish historian. Sometime Secretary for War and Paymaster-General. Wrote *A History of England*.

MacBAIN, Sir James (1828-92) of Ross-shire. Statesman and cabinet minister. He was a director of two Banks and three Insurance Offices.

MacCAIG, Norman (1910-) of Edinburgh. Poet. His many works include 'Riding Lights' (1957), 'Rings on a Tree' (1968), 'A Man in My Position' (1969) and 'The White Bird' (1973).

MacCALL, Charles J. (1907-) of Edinburgh. Artist. Painter of portraits, landscapes and contemporary life. Exhibited regularly in London and in one-man shows in Leicester, Dublin, New York, Manchester and Montreal.

McCALL, Sir Henry W. U. (1895-) of Ayrshire. Admiral (1953). Naval Attaché, Buenos Aires (1938-40), Senior British Naval Officer, Middle East (1956-48), Flag Officer Destroyers, Mediterranean Fleet (1949-50).

McCALLUM, David (1933-) of Glasgow. Actor best known for his starring roles in TV's *The Man from UNCLE* and *Colditz.*

McCLINTOCK, Sir Francis L. (1819-1907). Admiral and Polar explorer. Was knighted for discovering the fate of the Franklin expedition.

MacCOLL, Dugald Sutherland (1859-1948) of Glasgow. Painter, poet and art historian. Keeper of the Tate Gallery (1906-11) and of the Wallace Collection (1911-24).

McCRAE, John (1872-1918), born in Ontario of Scottish parents. Doctor and poet. When a medical officer in the Great War, wrote 'Flanders Fields' one of the great war poems which appeared in 1915.

MacCULLOCH, Sir James (1819-) of Glasgow. Politician who became Prime Minister of Australia in 1863.

McCULLOCH, John Ramsay (1789-1864) of Whithorn. Political economist. In 1828 became Prof. of Political Economy, Univ. Coll., London, and Comptroller of HM Stationery Office in 1838.

MacCUNN, Hamish (1868-1916) of Greenock. Composer and song writer of remarkable individuality. He was conductor of the Carl Rosa and other opera companies and professor of Composition at the Guildhall School of Music.

McDONALD, Alexander (1903-) of Edinburgh. Secretary of the Institute of Civil Engineers (1954-). Director of Public Works, Sierra Leone (1942-43). Inspector-General of Public Works, Nigeria (1951-54).

MacDONALD, Angus Alexander (1904-) of Edinburgh. Deputy Commissioner, Lyallpur (1933-36), Amritsar (1936-41), Deputy Home Sec., Punjab (1941-43) and Home Sec., Punjab (1943-47).

MacDONALD, Sir Claud (1852-1915). Sometime British Minister at Peking.

MacDONALD, Donald M. T. (1909-) of the Isle of Skye. Air-Vice Marshal, Director-General of Manning, Air Ministry (1956-61).

MacDONALD, Flora (1722-90) of Milton, South Uist. Disguised as 'Betty Burke' she conducted Prince Charles Edward Stewart to safety in Skye in 1746.

MacDONALD, George (1824-1905) of Huntly. Poet and novelist. *David Elginbrod* (1862), *The Marquis of Lossie* (1877) and *Sir Gibbie* (1879) are three of his best novels.

MacDONALD, Harry (1886-) of Isle of Skye. Major-General (1940), Was General Staff Officer, Western Commd., India (1928-31). Major-General, Cavalry, India (1939-40), and other high appointments in India.

MacDONALD, Sir Hector Archibald (1852-1903) of Dingwall. Soldier, who rose from the ranks and became a General, known as 'Fighting Mac'. Distinguished himself at Omdurman. It has been alleged that he had been involved in the Russo-Japanese War.

MacDONALD, Iverach (1908-) of Strathcool, Caithness. Associate editor of *The Times* newspaper (1967-68), and Director (1968-).

MacDONALD, Jacques Etienne Joseph Alexandre, Duc de Tarente (1765-1840). Born at Sudan of Scottish descent. Became Marshal of France after his defeat of the Austrians at Wagram in 1809.

MacDONALD James Ramsay (1866-1937) of Lossiemouth. First Labour Prime Minister of Britain in 1924 (Jan. to Nov.). Re-elected Prime Minister in 1929 and formed a National Government in 1931 during the financial crisis.

McDONALD, Sir John (1898-) son of Donald McDonald of Falkirk. Minister for Water Supply and Electricity in Victoria, Australia (1943-45), Minister for Lands, etc. (1947-48) and Premier and Treasurer, Victoria, Australia (1950-52).

MacDONALD, Sir John Alexander (1815-91) of Rogart, Sutherland. First Prime Minister of Canada (1856). He was mainly instrumental in bringing about the Confederation of Canada.

MacDONALD, Malcolm J. (1901-1981) of Lossiemouth. Son of Jas. Ramsay MacDonald. High Commissioner, Canada (1941-46), Governor-General, Malaya and Borneo (1946-48), Commissioner-General, SE Asia (1948-55), High Commissioner in India (1955-60) and Special Representative HM Govt. in Africa (1966-69). He was also Governor and C in C Kenya (1963).

MacDONALD, S. Douglas (1899-) of Glen Urquhart, Inverness-shire. Air Vice-Marshal, Head of Air Training Advisory Group NATO (1952-54).

MacDONALD, Thomas C. (1909-). Air Vice-Marshal (1961) and Principal Medical Officer, Tech. Training Commd., RAF (1961-66).

MacDONELL of Glengarry (Aeneas R. Donald). Air Commodore. Appointed Director of Management and Work Study, Ministry of Defence, Air Force Dept. in 1961.

MacDOUGALL, Alastair Ian (1888-). Son of late Col. Jas. Mac-Dougall of Edinburgh. Major-General (1940) (Ret. 1944) Commanded Royal Scots Greys (1928-32). General Staff, War Office (1936-39). Deputy Chief of General Staff (1940).

MacDOUGALL, Alexander (1731-) of Islay. Major-General in the American Revolutionary War. Was a delegate to the Continental Congress in 1780 and 1784.

MacDOUGALL, Sir David (1912-) of Glasgow. Head of Govt. Economic Service and Chief Economic Adviser to the Treasury (1969-).

McDOUGALL, John B. (1890-1967) of Greenock. Sometime chief of the Tuberculosis Section, World Health Organisation, Geneva and Consultant in Tuberculosis to the Egyptian Govt.

McEACHERN, Sir Malcolm Donald (1852-1910) of Islay. Shipowner. Made Mayor of the city of Melbourne in 1899.

McEWEN, Sir John B. (1868-1948) of Hawick. Composer and Principal of the Royal College of Music, London (1924-36).

MacEWEN, Sir William (1848-1924) of Rothesay. Surgeon and pioneer in brain, lung and orthopaedic surgery. He was the first to operate for a brain abcess (1876) and successfully removed a brain tumor in 1878. He was also the first to perform a complete removal of a lung for tuberculosis in 1895.

McFADZEAN, Francis Scott, Baron (Life Peer) (1913-) of Glasgow. As Chairman of Shell Transport and Trading was Britain's highest paid businessman. Chairman of British Airways (1976-79) and of Rolls Royce from 1979.

McFADZEAN, William H., Baron (Life Peer) (1903-) of Stranraer. Chairman British Insulated Callender Cables Ltd. (1954-). Director (1949) and Deputy Chairman (1968) Midland Bank, etc.

MacFARLANE, George G. (1916-) of Airdrie. Appointed Controller (research) Ministry of Technology in 1967.

MacFARQUHAR, Sir Alexander (1903-), educ. Aberdeen and Cambridge. Director of personnel, United Nations (1962-67) UN Sec-General's special adviser for civil affairs in the Congo (1960).

MacFARQUHAR, Colin (1745-93) of Edinburgh. Printer and co-founder of the *Encyclopaedia Britannica*.

McGAW, William Rankin (1900-) of Glasgow. Director of Aircraft Equipment Production (1941), of Aircraft Supplies (General) (1946-48) and of Production (1948-52). Director-General, Aircraft Production, Min. of Supply (1952-61).

McGILL, Donald Fraser (1875-1962). His forebears emigrated to Canada from Wigtownshire. Originator of the popular, comic and saucy postcards. Hundreds of millions were produced.

McGILLIVRAY, Alexander (1759-93). Born in Georgia, USA. Son of Lachlan McGillivray of Inverness. Became a Red Indian Chief of the Creek tribe in 1777. He also became a colonel in the British army during the Revolution, and later a Brigadier-General in the US army.

McGILLIVRAY, William (1764-) of Inverness-shire. Fur trader. Founder of the Canadian town of Fort William on Lake Superior. In 1970 Fort William amalgamated with Port Arthur to form the new city of Thunder Bay.

McGONAGALL, William (1830-1902) of Edinburgh. Weaver and writer of doggerel verse.

McGREGOR, Alasdair Alpin (1899-1970). Educ. Tain, Inverness and Edin. Author and traveller. Explored MacDonnell Ranges in Central Australia (1952-53). Prolific writer, usually illustrated with his own photographs.

MacGREGOR, Sir Alexander S.M. (1881-1967) of Arbroath. Physician. Medical Officer of Health, Glasgow (1925-46). President, Society of Medical Officers of Health (1941-42).

MacGREGOR, Andrew (1897-) of Crieff. Air Vice-Marshal. Senior Air Staff Officer HQ No. 4 Gp.(1940-42), Air Officer Admin., North Africa (1942-44), AOC No.28 Gp.(1945-46) and AOA, HQ Fighter Commd. (1946-49).

MacGREGOR, Sir Gregor (-d.1845). A remarkable character who became a General in the Venezuelan army under Simon Bolivar.

MacGREGOR, J. Geddes, (1909-) son of the late Thos. Geddes MacGregor of Dundee. Dean of the Graduate School of Religion and Professor of Philosophy of Religion, Univ. of Southern California (1960-).

MacGREGOR, Sir Ian Kinloch (1912-) of Kinlochleven. Metallurgist. Left Scotland in 1941 to advise the Americans on steel for tanks and battleships. Appointed Chairman of British Steel (1980-83) and the

Coal Board in 1983 when he was instrumental in the breaking of the year long strike and the overpowering of the NUM.

McGREGOR, Sir James of Lethendrey, Strathspey. Surgeon and soldier. Was Wellington's Surgeon General. Became known as the 'Father of the Royal Army Medical Corps'.

MacGREGOR, Lewis R. (1886-) of Aberfeldy. Director-General Commonwealth of Australia War Supplies Procurement Mission, Washington and Ottawa (1941-45). HM Australian Minister to Brazil (1945-49).

MacGREGOR, Robert B. (1896-) educ. Dunbar and Edinburgh. Retired as Senior Medical Officer, Malacca Agricultural Medical Board in 1958. Sometime Director, Medical Services, Straits Settlements and Adviser, Medical Services, Malay States (1940-).

McGUGAN, Stuart, (1944-) of Stirling. Journalist who became an actor. Best known for his part in TVs *It Aint Half Hot Mum* and as a regular presenter of *Playschool*.

MacHABENS, Johannes (-d.1557). A reformer of the clan MacAlpine, who from 1542 was Professor of Theology at Copenhagen.

McHARDY, William D. (1911-) of Banffshire. Professor of Hebrew, Oxford Univ. (1960-). Examiner, Univs. of Aberdeen, Cambridge, Durham, Edinburgh, Leeds, London, Oxford and Gold Coast Univ. Coll.

MacILWRAITH, Sir Thomas (1835-1900) of Ayr. Politician who was Premier of Queensland, Australia (1879-86, 1888 and 1892-93).

MacINNES, Helen C., of Helensburgh ? Author. Wrote many novels incl. *Above Suspicion* (1941), *The Unconqurable, Friends and Lovers* (1947) and *North From Rome* (1958).

McINTOSH, Alastair (1913-) of Dundee. Principal Adviser to the High Commissioner, Aden, (1963-64).

MacINTOSH, Charles (1766-1843) of Glasgow. Chemist and inventor. He obtained a patent (1825) for converting malleable iron into steel, thus helping Neilson to bring in his 'hot-blast' process (1828). He patented his misnamed Mackintosh waterproof cloth in 1823. Elected FRS (1823).

MacINTOSH, Duncan W. (1904-) of Inverness. Was Commissioner of Police, Hong Kong (1946-54), and Police Adviser to the Govt. of Iraq (1954-58) and to Govt. of Jordan (1962-).

MacINTOSH, Capt. William (? -d.1825). Son of Benjamin MacIntosh of Borlum, Inverness-shire. Became a Red Indian Chief of the Creek tribe.

MacINTYRE, Sir Donald (1891-) of Glasgow. Minister of Finance, Federation of Rhodesia and Nyasaland (1953-62). Made a Freeman of the city of Bulawayo in 1955.

MacIVER, Robert Morrison (1882-1970) of the Isle of Lewis. Professor of Political Philosophy and Sociology, Columbia Univ. (1929-50). Director, New York City Juvenile Delinquency Evaluation Project (1956-61) and President of the New School of Social Research (1963-65).

MacKAIL, John William (1859-1945) of Bute. Classical scholar. Professor of Poetry at Oxford (1906-11). President of the British Academy (1932-33) *Latin Literature–a Survey of the Whole Literature of Ancient Rome* (1895) was his work.

MacKAY Alexander Morehead (1849-90) of Rhynie, Aberdeenshire. Engineer and pioneer missionary to Uganda (1875-90) Became known as 'MacKay of Uganda'. Died of a fever at Usumbiro.

MacKAY, Charles (1814-89) of Perth. Songwriter, and editor of the *Illustrated London News* (1848-59). New York correspondent of *The Times* during the Civil War (1862-65). Two of his songs 'There's a Good Time coming' and 'Cheer Boys Cheer' were extremely popular.

MacKAY, Dave, (1934-) of Edinburgh. Footballer, team trainer and manager of outstanding ability. Became known as the 'Iron Man' of football. He had 22 Scottish Caps. Surely one of Scotland's football all-time greats.

MacKAY, Fulton (1923-87) of Paisley. Actor. Played many major parts in TV productions including, *The Master of Ballantrae, Special Branch, Porridge,* and *Some Mothers do 'ave em.*

MacKAY, Sir Gordon (1914-) of Aberdeenshire. General Manager, East African Railways and Harbours (1961-64). With the World Bank (1965-).

MacKAY, Hugh (c.1640-92) of Scourie, Sutherland. General who fought for Charles II after the Restoration (1660) and then for France against Holland. He later attached himself to William of Orange (1689).

MacKAY James, Scottish botanist who discovered the sources of the Mississippi and Missouri rivers in 1784.

MacKAY, James, Lord MacKAY of Clashfern (1927-) Edinburgh. Appointed Lord Chancellor in 1987. Noted for his legal reforms in Britain's complicated legal system. Not all of his reforms are popular with English lawyers.

MacKAY Sir John (1912-) of Blantyre. Became Chief Inspector of Constabulary for England and Wales. Was Chief Constable in Manchester (1959-66).

MacKAY, John A. (1889-) of Inverness. President of Princeton Theological Seminary (1936-59). Moderator, General Assembly of the Presbyterian Church in the USA (1953).

MacKAY, Mary (1855-1924) of Perth. Novelist who wrote under the name of 'Marie Corelli'. With *The Sorrows of Satan* (1895) she became the most popular novelist of her time in Britain.

McKELLAR, Kenneth (1927-) of Paisley. Singer and concert artist. Principal tenor, Carl Rosa Opera Co. (1953-54). His TV and radio programme *A Song for Everyone* was well received. Has had several successful Commonwealth tours.

MacKENZIE, Alexander (1822-92) of Dunkeld, Perthshire. Canadian statesman. Became Prime Minister of Canada after Sir John Mac-Donald (1873-78).

MacKENZIE, Sir Alexander (1764-1820) of Stornoway. Explorer and fur-trader in NW Canada. The MacKenzie River which bears his name was discovered by him in 1789. He crossed the Rockies to the Pacific (1792-93).

MacKENZIE, Sir Alexander Campbell (1847-1935) of Edinburgh. Composer and conductor. Conductor of the Philharmonic Society (1892-99). President of the International Music Society (1908-12). Composed many notable works including *The Cricket on the Hearth* (1914), *The Eve of St John* (1924) and the oratorio *The Rose of Sharon* (1884).

MacKENZIE, Charles Frederick (1825-62) of Peeblesshire. Became the first Anglican Bishop in Central Africa.

MacKENZIE, Colin (1755-1821) of Stornoway. Colonel and surveyor. A brilliant mathematician. Became first Surveyor-General of India in 1815.

MacKENZIE, Sir George (1636-91) of Dundee. Lawyer, writer and politician. Held the post of Lord-Advocate under Charles II and James II. As criminal prosecutor in the days of the Covenanters he earned the name 'bluedy Mackenzie'.

MacKENZIE, Sir George S. (1780-1848). Minerologist. He was first to obtain proof of the identity of diamond with carbon.

MacKENZIE Henry (1745-1831) of Edinburgh. Novelist, essayist and lawyer. Perhaps best remembered as a writer. His most famous work was *The Man of Feeling* (1771).

MacKENZIE, Sir Hugh (1913-) of Inverness. Vice-Admiral, Flag Officer Submarines (1961-63). Director, Atlantic Salmon Research Trust (1959-).

MacKENZIE, Sir James (1853-1925) of Scone, Perthshire. Physician. In 1902 he published his classical *Study of the Pulse*. He invented the polygraph to record graphically the heart's action. His *Diseases of the Heart* (1908) confirmed his reputation as one of the world's greatest cardiologists. Elected FRS in 1915.

MacKENZIE, Sir Morell (1837-92). Physician and throat specialist. Co-founder of the Hospital for Diseases of the Throat, London.

MacKENZIE, Sir Robert (1811-) of Ross-shire. Became Prime Minister of Australia in 1869.

MacKENZIE, William Lyon (1795-1861) of Dundee. Journalist, reformer and patriot. Leader of the Upper Canadian rebellion of 1837-38. He became first Mayor of Toronto in 1834. Elected to the Legislature of Canada in 1851.

MacKENZIE, William W. (1860-1923) of Scone. Lawyer and industrial arbitrator. Chairman, Rly. National Wages Bd. (1920-26), Royal Commission on licensing (1929-31) and on Newfoundland (1935). Chairman, Royal Society of Arts (1937-38).

MacKINNON, Donald M. (1913-) of Oban. Professor of Divinity, Cambridge Univ. (1960-). Lecturer on philosophy and religion.

MacKINNON, Quintin (-d.1892) of Argyll. Surveyor and explorer. Discovered MacKinnon's Pass in New Zealand about 1888.

MacKINNON, Sir William (1823-93) of Campbeltown, Argyll. Founder of the British East Africa Co. In 1878 following negotiations with the Sultan of Zanzibar, MacKinnon secured by lease, large strips of the East African coast for Great Britain.

MacKINTOSH, Angus M. (1915-) of Inverness. Sometime British High Commissioner in Ceylon. Ambassador to the Republic of Maldives (1969-).

MacKINTOSH, Charles Rennie (1868-1928) of Glasgow. Architect and decorative designer who exercised considerable influence on European design. The Scottish Pavilion at the Turin Exhibition (1902) was his work, as was Queen's Cross Church, Glasgow.

MacKINTOSH, Elizabeth (-d.1952) of Inverness. Novelist and playwright. Her best known novel *Kip* (1929) was written under her pen-name 'Gordon Daviot'.

MacKINTOSH, Sir James (1765-1832) of Aldowrie, Loch Ness. Journalist, historian, philosopher and statesman. Was Professor of Law at East India Coll., Haileybury (1818-24).

MacLAREN, Charles (1782-1866) of Ormiston, E.Lothian. Writer and first editor of the *Scotsman*. Edited the *Encyclopaedia Britannica* (6th ed.)

MacLAREN, Sir Hamish (1898-) of Banffshire. Director of Electrical Engineering, Admiralty (1945-60).

McLAREN, Hugh C. (1913-) of Glasgow. Professor of Obstetrics and Gynaecology, Univ. of Birmingham (1951-).

McLAREN, John (1845-) of Bannockburn. Gardener who designed the Golden Gate Park in San Francisco.

McLAUGHLIN, John. A Scottish chemist in Toronto. Invented the popular soft drink 'Canada Dry' about 1890.

MacLAURIN, Colin (1698-1746) of Kilmodan, Argyll. Mathematician. His *Treatise on Fluxions* (1742) was of great importance. Was also the author of *A Treatise on Algebra*. Elected FRS in 1719.

MacLEAN, Alistair (1922-87) of Deviot, Inverness-shire. Novelist and playwright. Was Britain's best selling author, and one of the world's most successful adventure writers. *H.M.S. Ulysses*, *The Guns of Navarone* and *Where Eagles Dare* are but three of his many exciting books. Has had 13 of his novels made into films. Described himself as a businessman whose business is writing.

MacLEAN, Allan (1840-1911) Scottish statesman who became Premier and First Secretary of Victoria, Australia (1899-1900). Minister of Trade and Customs, Commonwealth Parliament of Australia (1904-05).

MacLEAN, Sir Charles H. Fitzroy, Baron (life peer). Chief Scout of the British Commonwealth and Empire (1959-71). The Lord Chamberlain, The Organiser of Princess Anne's wedding, The Queen's Silver Jubilee Celebration, Lord Mountbatten's Funeral and Prince Charles' Wedding.

MacLEAN, Donald M. (1899-) of the Isle of Lewis. Was Commodore Captain, Cunard Fleet and Commander RMS *Queen Elizabeth* (1960-62).

MacLEAN, Sir Fitzroy Hew (1911-) of Dunconnel. Diplomat and soldier. Distinguished himself as Commander of the British military mission to the Jugoslav partisans (1943-45).

MacLEAN, Sir Harry (Kaid) (c.1848-1920) of Mull. Sometime Commander in Chief of the Sultan of Morocco's Army.

McLEAN, Sir Kenneth G. (1896-). Educated in Edinburgh. Lieut.-General, Deputy Adjutant-General GHQ Far East (1945-46). Chief of Staff CCG and Deputy Military Governor British Zone, Germany (1949), Chief Staff Officer, Min. of Defence (1951-52).

MacLEHOSE, Crawford Murray, Lord MacLehose of Beoch, Ayrshire, (1917-) Diplomat, Governor and Commander in Chief, Hong Kong (1971-82), Ambassador to Vietnam (1967-69) and to Denmark (1969-71).

MacLELLAN, George D. (1922-) of Glasgow. Professor and Head of Engineering, Univ. of Liverpool (1965-). Visiting professor, Michigan State Univ. (1955-58).

MacLELLAN, Robert (1907-) of Lesmahago. Playwright. He wrote for the Citizen's Theatre and later for the BBC. His works incl. *The Changeling* (1935), *The Flowers O' Edinburgh* (1947) and *The Hypocrite* (1970).

MacLENNAN, Sir Ian (1909-) of Glasgow. Appointed British High Commissioner in New Zealand in 1964.

MacLEOD, Donald (Donny) (1932-) of Stornoway. TV Presenter on *Pebble Mill* (1973-), *Saturday Night at the Mill, The Best of Scottish,* etc.

MacLEOD, Very Revd George F. (Baron MacLeod of Fuinary). (1895-). Lecturer on Evangelism. First holder of Fosdick Professorship (Rockefeller Foundation), Union Theological Seminary, New York (1954-55).

MacLEOD, Ian Norman (1913-1970). Politician and Cabinet Minister. Minister of Health (1952-55) of Labour and National Service (1955-59), Sec. of State, Colonies (1959-61), Chairman, Conservative Party (1961-63), Editor of *The Spectator* (1964-65) and Chancellor of the Exchequer when he died.

MacLEOD, John James Rickard (1876-1935) of Cluny, near Dunkeld. Physiologist. Professor of Physiology at Cleveland, Ohio (1903-18), Toronto (1918-28). Celebrated for his work on the isolation of insulin, (1922) for which he won a Nobel Prize. His father belonged to Wick, Caithness.

MacLEOD, Norman (1812-72) of Campbeltown. Divine and writer. Appointed Chaplain to Queen Victoria in 1857.

MacMILLAN, Daniel (1813-57). Scottish publisher. Was employed as a bookseller in Irvine and Glasgow before moving to London where he became senior partner in the publishing business which was founded in 1843, now MacMillan Ltd.

MacMILLAN of MacMILLAN, Sir Gordon H. A. (1897-). General, GSO 2 War Office and Eastern Commd. (1937-40), GSI (1940-41), Brigade General Staff UK and N. Africa (1941-43), Commander Infantry Brigade, Sicily (1943), 15th Scottish and 51st Highland Divs. (1943-45), GOC Palestine (1947-48), C in C, Scottish Commd. and Gov. of Edinburgh Castle (1949-52) and Governor and C in C Gibraltar (1952-55).

MacMILLAN, Harold Earl MacMillan of Stockton (1894-1986), born in London, son of Daniel MacMillan, an Arran Crofter. Prime Minister of Gt. Britain (1957-63). The standard of living rose at a greater rate during his administration than at any other time in British history. Known as 'Super Mac' he is also remembered for his 'Wind of Change' warning on Africa in 1960.

MacMILLAN, Kenneth (1929-) Scottish choreographer and dancer. Director of the Royal Ballet (1970-77).

MacMILLAN, Kirkpatrick (1813-78) of Courthill, Dumfriesshire. Blacksmith. Invented the first bicycle to be propelled by cranks and pedals, about 1840. He was known locally as 'Daft Pate', and was an unofficial dentist who pulled teeth from both horses and men. A replica of his cycle can be seen in the Science Museum, South Kensington. He was fined 5/- (the first recorded fine for a cycle offence) for knocking over a child.

MacMILLAN, Margaret (1860-1931), born at Westchester, New York State of Scottish parents. Pioneer social worker and educationist. In 1923 she became the first president of the Nursery School Assoc., and in 1930 the Rachel MacMillan College was opened. It is now a constituent of the University of London Institute of Education.

MacMILLAN, Norman (1892-) of Glasgow. Author and test pilot. Was pilot of the first attempt to fly around the world in 1922, First flight London to Sweden in one day, Chief test pilot, Fairy Aviation Co. (1929-30) and Armstrong Siddeley Development Co. (1931-32). Produced many publications on flying.

MacMILLAN, Rachel (1859-1917) sister of Margaret MacMillan. Educationist. The Rachel MacMillan Training College bears her name.

MacMILLAN, Roddie (-d.1979) of Anderston, Glasgow. Actor on

screen and TV. Probably best remembered for his parts in TV's *Para Handy* and *The View from Daniel Pyke*.

MacMURRAY, John (1891-) of Maxwellton. Scholar and lecturer on philosophy, Univ. of Manchester (1919), Professor at Univ. of Witwatersrand, Johannesburg, and Professor of the Philosophy of Mind and Logic at the Univ. of London (1928-44).

MacNAB of MacNAB, Archibald C. (1886-1970). Commissioner at Rawalpindi (1934), Administrator, Jahore (1937), Commissioner, Jullundur (1940) and Financial Commissioner, Punjab (1945).

McNAIR, James Jamieson (1917-). Air Vice-Marshal (Ret.). Principal Medical Officer, HQ Support Commd. RAF (1974-77). Was Director of Health and Research, MOD (1971-74).

McNAUGHT, John (1813-81) of Paisley. Engineer and inventor of the compound steam engine.

McNEE, Sir David (1925-) of Glasgow. Commissioner of the Metropolitan Police (1977-82). He was made a Freeman of the City of London in 1977.

MacNEIL of BARRA (Robert Lister) (1889-1970). Chairman of Inventions Board, British Purchasing Commission, USA and founder of American Committee for Defence of British Homes (1939-45). Boston Univ. Resident Architect (1949-51).

McNEILL, Alister A. C. (1884-) of Glasgow. Major-General (1941). Hon. Surgeon to the King (1935-43).

McNEILL, Florence M. of Orkney. Author, journalist, lecturer and broadcaster.

McNEILL, Sir James, Chief designer of RMSs *Queen Mary* and *Queen Elizabeth* for John Brown of Clydebank.

McPETRIE, James Stewart (1902-) of Aberdeenshire. Director-General of Electronics Research and Development at Min. of Aviation (1958-62). Director, Racal Electronics (1965-69).

MacPHERSON, Sir David Lewis (1818-96) from Inverness-shire. Politician and Canadian Railway builder.

MacPHERSON, Sir Hubert Taylor (1827-86). Major-General at Tel-el-Kebir (1882).

MacPHERSON, James (1736-96) of Ruthven, near Kingussie. Poet and translator. Appointed Surveyor-General of the Florides (1764), and in 1779, Agent to the Nabob of Arcot. Buried in the 'Poet's Corner' of Westminster Abbey.

MacPHERSON, Sir John (1745-1821) of Sleat, Isle of Skye. Appointed

Governor-General of India in 1785.

McPHERSON, Sir John (1898-) of Edinburgh. Colonial servant and businessman. Governor of Nigeria (1948-54) and Gov.-General, Federation of Nigeria (1954-55). Permanent Under-Sec. of State for the Colonies (1956-59).

MacQUARIE, Lachlan (1761-1824) of Isle of Ulva. Major-General and Governor of New South Wales, Australia (1809-21). Sometimes affectionately called the 'father of Australia'.

MacRAE, James (c.1674-1744) of Ochiltree, Ayrshire. Seaman who became Governor of Madras (1725-31).

McROBERT, Sir George R. (1895-) of Aberdeen. Consulting physician, Hosp. for Tropical Diseases, London Univ. Coll. Hospital.

MacTAGGART, Sir George R. (1895-) of Ayrshire. Civil engineer. Was responsible for the construction of hydroelectric developments in Italy, India and East Africa, and the construction of large irrigation and railway works in Iraq.

McTAGGART, William (1835-1910) of Machrihanish. Artist and landscape painter.

MacTAGGART, Sir William (1903-81). Grandson of William McTaggart. Artist. President of RSA (1959-).

McVEY, Sir Daniel (1892-) of Falkirk. Sometime chairman, Dunlop Rubber Australia Ltd., and British Aircraft Corp. (Australia) Ltd., and several other companies.

McVITTIE, George C. (1904-), educated Edinburgh and Cambridge. Professor of Astronomy, Univ. of Illinois (1952-). Sec. American Astronomical Society (1961-). Published several books on cosmology.

McWHIRTER, Norris Dewar (1925-). Author, publisher and broadcaster. Director, Guinness Superlatives Ltd. since 1954; (Managing Director 1954-56).

McWHIRTER, Robert (1904-) of Glasgow ? Professor of Medical Radiology. Lecturer, American Roentgen Ray Society (1963).

MAIN, Alexander, a Scot who in 1839 invented a soot distributing machine which became the first mechanical means of distributing dry fertiliser.

MAIR, William (1830-1920) of Aberdeenshire. Divine and writer. A pioneer in church reunion.

MAIR, George B. (1914-) of Mauchline, Ayrshire. Surgeon and author. His admission that he had practised euthanasia caused a sensation when his book *Confessions of a Surgeon* appeared in 1974.

MAITLAND, Alastair G. (1916-). Director-General of Trade Development, British Consulate, New York (1968-).

MAITLAND, Donald J. Dundas (1922-) of Edinburgh. Ambassador to Libya (1969-70), Chief of Downing St. Press Office (1970-73) and British representative on UN Security Council (1973-).

MAITLAND, Sir Richard (1496-1586) of Lethington. Poet, lawyer and historian. His poetic works consisted mostly of laments for the State of Scotland, the feuds of the nobles and the discontents of the common people. Was made Lord Privy Seal in 1562.

MALCOLM, Sir John (1769-1833) of Burnfoot, Langholm. General, administrator, diplomat and writer. Envoy to Persia (1800, 1807 and 1810). Governor of Bombay (1826-30). He wrote *Political History of India* (1811), *History of Persia* (1818) and *Administration of India* (1833). Buried in Westminster Abbey.

MANSON, George (1850-76) of Edinburgh. Painter and wood engraver.

MANSON, Sir Patrick (1844-1922) of Oldmeldrum. Known as the father of tropical medicine. The first, jointly with Sir Ronald Ross, to discover that parasites were transmitted by insects. He was sometimes known as 'Mosquito Manson'.

MAR, John Erskine, 11th Earl of (1675-1756). Scottish Jacobite famed as the leader of the 1715 rebellion.

MARGARET, Saint (1045-93). Scottish saint and Queen. Married Malcolm III in 1070. Deeply religious she influenced her husband to reform abuses in the church.

MARSHALL, William Calder (1813-94) of Edinburgh. Sculptor (RA 1852). Famed for busts and memorial statues, including the group *Agriculture* on the Albert Memorial.

MARTELL, Lena (1959-) of Glasgow. Popular singer who has appeared in all the best clubs in Britain. She has also appeared in the London Palladium, London's Festival Hall, and in Hong Kong, South Africa, Australia and Canada. Lena Martell has written more than 30 songs.

MARTIN, Martin (?-d.1719) of Skye. Author and traveller. His book *A Description of the Western Isles* aroused Dr Johnson's interest in Scotland.

MARTIN, Sir Theodore (1816-1909) of Edinburgh. Lawyer and author. Became a parliamentary solicitor in London. Was requisitioned by Queen Victoria to write the *Life of the Prince Consort* (5 vols. 1875-80).

MARY, QUEEN of SCOTS (1542-87). Queen of Scotland and Queen-Consort of France. Mary was a Queen before she was a week old. She was beheaded in 1587 after Elizabeth I of England signed her death warrant.

MASSON, David (1822-1907) of Aberdeen. Scholar and literary critic. The biographer of Milton. His *Life of John Milton* (6 vols. 1859-80) has been described as the most complete biography of any Englishman.

MATTHEW, Sir Robert Hogg (1906-75) of Edinburgh. Architect. From 1946 to 1953 he was architect to the London County Council. Was joint designer of the Royal Festival Hall (1951). His buildings incl. New Zealand House (1958-63) and the Commonwealth Institute (1959-62).

MATTHEWS, James (1889-) of Perthshire. Professor of Botany, Univ. of Reading (1929-34), Univ. of Aberdeen and Keeper of Cruickshank Botanic Gardens (1934-59).

MAXTON, James (1885-1946) of Glasgow. Politician. Chairman, Independent Labour Party (1926).

MAXWELL, Sir Aymer (1891-) of Kirkcudbrightshire. Major-General (ret. 1944). Chairman, British Legion, Scotland (1954-58). Member of the Queen's Bodyguard for Scotland (the Royal Company of Archers).

MAXWELL, James Clerk (sometimes Clerk-Maxwell) (1831-79) of Galloway. Physicist. First Professor of Experimental Physics at Cambridge (1871). He first forecast the possibility of radio transmission (1865), invented automatic control system (1868) and was creator of the electromagnetic theory of light. Described as the father of modern science, he was one of Scotland's greatest sons.

MAXWELL, Robert, Lord (c.1493-1546) of Edinburgh. Statesman and member of the Royal Council under James V. He was also an extraordinary Lord of Session in 1533 and one of the Regents in 1536.

MAXWELL, Sir William G. C. (1882-1965) son of George Maxwell of New Galloway. Rear Admiral (1934). Recalled as Flag Officer, Tyne Area (1939-46).

MEIKE, David E.C. (1902-) of Edinburgh. Professor of Clinical Surgery, Univ. of Malaya (1935-55). Surgeon, Singapore General Hosp. and Hon. Surgical Consultant, Far East Command.

MEIKLE, Andrew (1719-1811) from near Dunbar. A prolific inventor. Fantail gear (1750) and governing sails for windmills (1772), Grain dressing machine (1768) and a Drum threshing machine (1784) were only four of his inventions.

MELVILLE, Andrew (1545-1622) of Montrose. Presbyterian theologian and religious reformer. Was Professor of Humanity at Geneva Academy (1568-74). He was repeatedly Moderator of the Church Assembly of the Church of Scotland. He helped to bring about the fall of episcopacy in Scotland.

MELVILLE, Archibald (1912-) of Edinburgh. Was appointed Director of Agriculture, Kenya in 1960.

MELVILLE, Sir Harry (1908-) of Edinburgh. Appointed Sec. to the Committee of the Privy Council for Scientific and Industrial Research in 1956. Member, Governing Bd. of National Institute for Research in Nuclear Science (1957-).

MELVILLE, Herman (1819-91), New York son of a Scottish merchant. Novelist and poet. Remembered for his famous *Moby Dick* (1851), which came to be regarded as one of the greatest novels of American literature.

MELVILLE, Sir James (c.1535-1617) of Hallhill, Fife. Historical writer and diplomat. A member of the household of Mary, Queen of Scots, he carried out various missions for her.

MELVILLE, James (1556-1614) of Montrose. Reformer, tutor and professor of oriental languages.

MELVILLE, Thomas (1726-53) of Glasgow. Scientist. Was the first (1752) to study the spectra of luminous gases.

MENZIES, Andrew. Was the inventor of horse and manpowered coal cutting machines in 1863.

MENZIES, Sir Laurence J. (1906-) of Cupar Angus. In 1957 he was appointed Adviser to the Governors of the Bank of England.

MENZIES, Michael (d.1766) of East Lothian. Advocate and inventor. Was the first to suggest thrashing grain with a machine. He invented the first mechanical thrasher in 1734. A water-powered machine driving a number of whirling flails. In 1750 he invented a machine for conveying coal from the coal face to the bottom of the pit shaft.

MENZIES, Sir Robert (1891-1967) of Edinburgh. President Upper India Chamber of Commerce (1939-41 and 1944-45), Chairman, Federation of Woollen Manufacturers in India (1941-47) and other companies.

MENZIES, Sir Robert Gordon (1897-1969) of Japarit, Australia, of Scottish descent. Prime Minister of Australia (1939-41 and 1949-66).

MENZIES, Thomas (1893-1969) of Aberdeenshire. Professor of Tropical Medicine, Royal Army Medical Coll. (1940). Major-General

(1949). Served in RAMC in 1914-18 and 1939-45 wars. Director of Medical Services, GHQ MELF (1948-50). Hon. Physician to the King (1949-52).

MERCER, Sir Walter (1890-) of Midlothian. Professor of Orthopaedic Surgery and Fellow, Royal Soc. of Medicine and Assoc. of Surgeons, Gt. Britain and Ireland.

MICHIE, Charles W. (1907-) of Aberdeenshire. Permanent Sec. to N.Region, Min. of Agriculture in Nigeria (1957-60). Consul for Spanish Territories of Gulf of Guinea, and Labour Officer, Nigerian Dept. of Labour (1940- 42).

MICKLE, William Julius (1735-88) of Langholm. Poet. Best remembered for 'There's nae Luck Aboot the Hoose'.

MILL, James (1773-1836) from near Montrose. Philosopher, editor, and writer. Wrote *History of British India* (1817-18). Appointed Asst. Examiner in Charge of the Revenue Dept. of the East India Co. (1819) and in 1832 head of the Examiner's Office where he had control of all the departments of Indian administration.

MILL IRVING, David J. (1904-) of Edinburgh. Ambassador to Costa Rica (1956-61). Special Ambassador for the inauguration of the President of Honduras (1957) and of Costa Rica (1958).

MILLAR, Betsy (1793-1864) of Saltcoats, Ayrshire. First woman ever to be registered at Lloyd's as a ship's captain.

MILLAR, Patrick (1731-1815) from near Dumfries. Inventor and projector of steam navigation.

MILLAR of ORTON, Robert Kirkpatrick (1901-) of Morayshire. Major-General, Commanded Royal Engineers 15th (Scottish) Div. (1942-43) in France and Germany. Chief Engineer, London District (1949-51), Scottish Commd. (1951-53) Engineer in Chief, Pakistan Army (1953-57).

MILLER, Hugh (1802-56) of Cromarty. Stonemason and geologist, writer and editor. *Old Red Sandstone* (1841) is considered his best geological work.

MILLER, Sir James (1905-1977) of Edinburgh. Architect. Lord Provost of Edinburgh (1951-54) and Lord Mayor of London (1964-65).

MILLER, James (1812-64) of Eassie, Forfarshire. Surgeon. Professor of Surgery at Edinburgh Univ. (1842-64). One of the foremost surgeons of his day.

MILLER, Maxwell of Glasgow. In 1850 he invented an improved still for distilling and rectifying spirits.

MILLER, William (1810-72) of Glasgow. Poet best remembered for his poem 'Wee Willie Winkie'. He was called the 'Laureate of the nursery'.
MILLER, William (1838-1923) of Thurso. Missionary to India. Founder of Madras Christian College.
MILN, James (1819-81). Antiquary. Made excavations at a Roman site at Carnac, Brittany (1872-80). Miln Museum, Carnac contains the collection.
MILNE, Alasdair (1930-) born in India, son of an Aberdeen surgeon. Director-General of the BBC (1982-87) Controller BBC Scotland (1968-72), Director of programmes BBC TV (1973-77) and Managing Director BBC TV (1977-82).
MILNE, Alexander (1891-) of Skene, Aberdeenshire. Engineer, engaged from 1927 on opening up and development of Cochin Harbour, S.India. Chief Engineer Cochin Harbour (1941-48).
MILNE, Sir David (1763-1845) of Edinburgh. Admiral, known as 'The Hero of Algiers'. Was C in C Plymouth (1842-45).
MILNE, William (1785-1822) of Kinnethmont, Aberdeenshire. Missionary in China.
MILNE, William (1815-63) son of the above William. Was also a missionary in China.
MILNE, William P. (1881-1967) of Longside, Aberdeenshire. Was Professor of Mathematics at the Univ. of Leeds (1919-46).
MILNE HENDERSON, Thomas M. S. (1888-1968) of Edinburgh. Surveyor in charge of Marine Survey of India (1930-35). Appointed Capt. Supt., HM Indian Naval Dockyard, Bombay and Chief of Staff RIN in 1937.
MINTO, Gilbert Elliot, 1st Earl of (1751-1814) of Edinburgh. Governor-General of India (1807-13), a post he held with great ability.
MINTO, Gilbert John Elliot, 4th Earl of (1845-1914). Soldier and administrator. He was Governor-General of Canada (1898-1904) and Viceroy of India (1905-10).
MINTO, William (1845-93) of Alford, Aberdeenshire. Critic and biographer. Went to London and became editor of *The Examiner*. He also wrote for the *Daily News* and *Pall Mall Gazette*.
MITCHELL, Arthur J. (1893-1967) of Montrose. Civil Engineer, Director, Colonial Development Corp. (1949-51). Regional Controller, CDC for Central Africa and the High Commission Territories (1951-53).

MITCHELL, Sir Peter Chalmers (1864-1945) of Dunfermline. Biologist, Zoologist and writer. Sec. of the Zoological Soc. of London (1903-35). His publications incl. *Outlines of Biology* (1894), *The Nature of Man* (1903) and *The Childhood of Animals* (1912).

MITCHELL, Sir Thomas Livingstone (1792-1855) of Craigend, Stirlingshire. Explorer and surveyor. Surveyor-General of New South Wales (1828-). In four expeditions (1831, 1835, 1845 and 1847) he did much to explore eastern and tropical Australia.

MITCHISON, Naomi M., of Edinburgh. Novelist. *The Conquered* (1923), *When the Bough Breaks* (1924) and *Cloud Cuckoo Land* are three of her best works.

MOFFAT, James (1890-1944) of Glasgow. Theologian. Held professorships at Mansfield Coll., Oxford (1911-14), the U.F. Church Coll., Glasgow (1914-27) and the Union Theological Seminary, New York (1927-39). He translated the Bible into modern English.

MOFFAT, Robert (1795-1883) of Ormiston, E.Lothian. Missionary and explorer in Africa. He printed both New (1840) and Old (1857) Testaments in Sechwana language. David Livingstone married his daughter.

MOIR, John C. (1900-) of Montrose. Professor of Obstetrics and Gynaecology at the Univ. of Oxford (1937-). Was visiting professor, Queen's Univ., Ontario (1950).

MOLESWORTH, Mary Louisa (1839-1921), born at Rotterdam of Scottish descent, her maiden name being Stewart. Novelist and writer of children's books. *The Carved Lion* (1895) considered by many to have been her best. In all she wrote over a hundred books.

MOLLISON, James Allan (1905-59) of Glasgow. Airman. Won fame for his record flight, Australia to England in 1931. Made the first solo East-West crossing of the North Atlantic in 1932, and in 1933 the first England to South America flight.

MONBODDO, (James Burnett) Lord (1714-99) of Kincardinshire. Judge, philosopher and philologist. Wrote *An Essay on the Origin and Progress of Language* (6 vols. 1773-92) and *Ancient Metaphysics* (6 vols. 1779-99). He argued man's affinity to the orang-outang, and this in a way anticipated Darwin's theory.

MONCRIEFF, Sir Alexander (1829-1906) of Perthshire. Soldier and inventor. In 1868 he invented and developed the 'Moncrieff pit, or disappearing system'. A method of mounting heavy guns in coastal batteries. The gun disappearing after firing and reappearing when required through the use of stored recoil energy.

MONRO, Alexander (1), (1697-1767) Scottish anatomist. One of the founders of the Edinburgh Infirmary.

MONRO, Alexander (2), (1733-1817) of Edinburgh, son of (1). Anatomist. His most important work was his *Observations on the Structure and Function of the Nervous System* (1783). He wrote on the physiology of fish (1785) and on the brain, eye, and ear (1797). Was the first (1767) to describe the use of a stomach tube.

MONRO, Alexander (3), (1773-1859) son of (2). Anatomist, succeeded his father. Wrote on hernia, the stomach and human anatomy. Elected FRS of Edinburgh.

MONTGOMERIE, Alexander (c.1556-1610) of Ayrshire. Poet. In 1577 he became one of James VII's 'Castalian Band' of court poets. His chief poem is 'The Cherrie and the Slae' (1597) which contained many beautiful passages. Montgomerie also introduced the Sonnet to Scotland.

MONTGOMERY, James (1771-1854) of Irvine. Poet, hymn-writer and journalist. In 1810 he published a volume of verse *The West Indies* appealing for the abolition of the slave trade. He started and edited the *Sheffield Iris* (1794-1825). 'Forever with the Lord' was his best known hymn.

MONTGOMERY, Lucy Maud (1874-1942), born in Canada of Scottish descent. Novelist. Her first novel *Anne of Green Gables* (1908) was an international best seller.

MONTROSE, (James A. Graham) 7th Duke of, (1907-). Minister of Agriculture, Lands and Natural Resources in Southern Rhodesia (1964) and Minister of External Affairs and Defence, S. Rhodesia (1966-68).

MONTROSE (James Graham) 1st Marquis of (1612-50). 'The Great Montrose'. General and statesman. He also wrote a number of lyrics, the best known of which is 'My Dear and Only Love'. He was executed in Edinburgh.

MOODIE, Donald (-d.1861) of Melsetter, Orkney. Naval Commander. Was Colonial Secretary at Natal (1845-51).

MOORE, John (1729-1802) of Stirling. Novelist and surgeon. Moore's *Journal of a Residence in France* (1793) was made use of by Carlyle.

MOORE, Sir John (1761-1809) of Glasgow. General. Distinguished himself in the descent upon Corsica (1794). Served with great distinction in the West Indies (1796), Ireland (1798), Holland (1799), Egypt

(1801), Sicily and Sweden (1802) and Spain (1808-09).

MORAY, (James Stuart) Earl of (1531-70). Appointed Regent of Scotland (1567) and was one of the Commissioners sent to England to conduct negotiations against Mary, Queen of Scots.

MORISON, Robert (1620-83) of Aberdeen. Botanist and physician. Sometime in charge of the gardens of the Duke of Orleans. Charles II made him one of his physicians. Morison was Botanist Royal and Professor of Botany at Oxford.

MORRISON, Alexander (1917-), educ. Edinburgh. Controller of Services, Greater London Council (1970-). Executive Director Highways and Transportation (1967-69) and other appointments in equipment control and supply.

MORRISON, Charles, of Greenock. Surgeon who in 1753 was the first projector of the Electric Telegraph.

MORRISON, George (c.1704-99). Scottish General, Military Engineer and Quartermaster-General.

MORRISON, Dr G. E. (1862-1920). A scot who became known as 'Chinese Morrison' or 'Morrison of Peking'.

MORRISON, Peter (1940-) of Greenock. Lawyer and singing star. Made a name for himself on TV since 1971.

MORRISON, Robert (1782-1834) from near Jedburgh. Missionary. In 1818 he established the Anglo-Chinese College at Malacca. Completed in 1823 his great Chinese dictionary.

MORRISON, Stuart L. (1922-) of Glasgow. Professor of Social Medicine. Member of scientific staff, Medical Research Council, Social Research Unit (1956-62). Visiting fellow, Epidemiology and Statistics, Univ. of N. Carolina (1961-62).

MORTON, Thomas (1781-1832). Scottish shipbuilder and inventor (about 1822) of the patent slip which provided a cheap substitute for a dry dock.

MOTHERWELL, William (1797-1835) of Glasgow. Poet and journalist. His *Minstrelsy Ancient and Modern* (1827) was a collection of Scottish ballads with an historical introduction.

MOUNSEY Dr James of Lochmaben. Became Court physician to Catherine the Great of Russia. It was he who introduced rhubarb to Britain from Russia.

MOUNT STEVEN (George Steven) Baron (1829-1921) of Dufftown, Banffshire. Financier. Became President of the Bank of Montreal. In partnership with his cousin Donald Smith (later Lord Strathcona) he purchased the St Paul and Pacific Railway, and started the construction of the Canadian Pacific Railway, which was completed in 1885.

MOWAT, Sir Oliver (1820-1903) son of John Mowat a Freswick, Caithness soldier. A great advocate of the union of Canada into a dominion. Premier and Attorney-General of Ontario (1872-96) and Lieut.-Governor (1897-).

MOWAT, Robert A. (1843-1925) Scotsman who became a Judge of the Court of HBM of Japan in 1891.

MUIR, Edwin (1887-1959) of Deerness, Orkney. Poet, novelist, translater and biographer. Son of a crofter, he became Professor of Poetry at Harvard, USA. He is acknowledged as one of Scotland's most distinguished poets of the twentieth century.

MUIR, Ernest (1880-) educ. Edinburgh. Medical missionary to U.F. Church in Kalna, Bengal (1905-20), Medical Supt., Leper settlement, Chacachacare (1904-45).

MUIR, John (1838-1914) of Dunbar. Naturalist, inventor, explorer and conservationist. Became known as 'Father of United States Conservation'. His inventions incl. a self-setting water powered sawmill, various locks, hygrometers, pyrometers, clocks, etc.

MUIR, John C. (1902-). Senior Agricultural Officer, Zanzibar (1935), Director of Agriculture, Zanzibar (1941), Trinidad (1944) and Tanganyika (1948).

MUIRHEAD, John Henry (1855-1940) of Glasgow. Philosopher. Editor of *Library of Philosophy* (1890) and professor at Mersey Coll., Birmingham (1897-1921).

MUNRO, Ferguson R., Viscount Novar (1860-). Governor-General of Australia (1914-18).

MUNRO, Sir Hector (1726-1805) of Novar. Soldier and General who distinguished himself in India.

MUNRO, Hugh A.J. (1819-95) of Elgin. Classical scholar. Professor of Latin at Cambridge (1869-72). His greatest achievement was an edition of *Locretius*.

MUNRO, Neil (1864-1930) of Inveraray. Novelist, poet and journalist. Editor of *Glasgow Evening News* (1918-27). Wrote a number of historical novels incl. *Doom Castle* (1901) and *Children of the Tempest* (1903). Probably best remembered for his *Para Handy* series, beginning with the *Vital Spark* (1906).

MUNRO, Robert (1835-1920). Scottish archaeologist. His writings incl., *Lake Dwellings of Scotland* (1882), *Lake Dwellings of Europe*

(1890) *Lake Dwellings of Bosnia* (1896) and *Prehistoric Britain* (1914).

MUNRO, Sir Thomas (1761-1827) of Glasgow. Soldier and Governor. Rendered good service to General Wellesley (later Duke of Wellington). Appointed Governor of Madras in 1819, a post he held for seven years with marked success. He promoted the education of natives and championed their rights.

MUNRO, William (1900-) of Kilmarnock. Queen's Counsellor. Called to the Bar in the Straits Settlement (1927), Jehore, Singapore, and Malaya (1927-57).

MURCHISON, Sir Roderick Impey (1792-1871) of Tarradale, Ross-shire. Geologist. His establishment of the Silurian system won him European fame. In 1844 he foreshadowed the discovery of gold in Australia. Was President of the British Assoc. in 1846 and appointed Director-General of the Geographical Survey and Royal School of Mines in 1855.

MURCHLAND, William of Kilmarnock. Patented a vacuum milking machine in 1889, using a column of water to create a vacuum.

MURDOCH, Sir Walter (1874-1970) of Aberdeenshire. Chancellor of the Univ. of Western Australia (1943-47), Lecturer at the Univ. of Melbourne and leader writer in the *Melbourne Argus*.

MURE, Sir William (1594-1657) of Rowallan, Ayrshire. Poet. Wrote *The True Crucifixe for True Catholikes* (1629), and a fine version of the Psalms (1639).

MURDOCK (originally Murdoch) William, (1754-1839) of Bello Mill, Old Cumnock, Ayrshire. A prolific inventor. In 1785 he invented a steam tricycle, gas lighting from coal (1796-1803), a steam cannon (1803), worm-driven cylinder-boring machine (1810) and a crown-saw boring machine. He also perfected underwater paint for ships. By trade he was a miller and millwright.

MURRAY, Alexander (1775-1813) of Kirkcudbright. Philologist who acquired a mastery of the classics. Became Minister of Urr (in 1806) and Professor of Oriental languages, Edinburgh (1812).

MURRAY, Charles (1864-1941) of Alford, Aberdeenshire. Poet and civil engineer. Was for some time, chief engineer and secretary for Public Works in the Union of South Africa. His poems in Aberdeenshire dialect were locally popular.

MURRAY, Charles (Chic) (-1985) Thomas McKinnon, of Greenock. Comedian on stage and TV.

MURRAY, Colin R. B. (1892-) of Ross-shire. Deputy Director of Intelligence, Govt. of India (1938) and Inspector-General of Police, Orissa, India (1944-46).

MURRAY, Sir David (1849-1933) of Glasgow. Painter noted for his paintings of Scottish landscapes and Italian lakes. Elected RA 1905.

MURRAY, Lord George (c.1700-60). Jacobite general. Son of the Duke of Atholl. Joined the 'Young Pretender' in 1745 and was one of his generals.

MURRAY, Sir George (1772-1846) of Crieff. General statesman and writer. Sec. of State for the Colonies (1828-30). Was Major-General of the Ordnance till his death. Elected FRS in 1824.

MURRAY, Sir Horatius (1903-) General. Served with distinction in N. Africa, Sicily, Italy and France (1939-45). Commander, Commonwealth Div. in Korea (1953-54), GOC in C Scottish Commd. and Governor of Edinburgh Castle (1955-58). C in C Allied Forces, Northern Europe (1958-61).

MURRAY, James (c.1719-94) of Edinburgh. General. Became Governor of Quebec and of Minorca. Governor of Canada (1763-66).

MURRAY or Murray Pultney, Sir James (c.1713-1811) of Fifeshire. (7th Baronet of Clermont). General and statesman.

MURRAY, James (1919-) of Isle of Arran. First Sec. (Information) British Embassy, Cairo (1949-54), Paris (1957-61). Ambassador to Rwanda and Burundi (1962-63). Consul-General, San Francisco (1970-).

MURRAY, Sir James Augustus Henry (1837-1915) of Denholm, nr. Hawick. Philologist and Lexicographer. The editing of the Philological Society's *New English Dictionary* (1879-1928) was the great work of his life.

MURRAY, James Dalton (1911-) of Edinburgh. Appointed British High Commissioner in Jamaica in 1965. Ambassador to Haiti (1966-).

MURRAY James Greig (1919-). Educated Peterhead, Aberdeen and Edinburgh. Professor of Surgery at the Univ. of London (Ret.). Produced many publications on surgery.

MURRAY, John (1), (1745-93) (originally McMurray) of Edinburgh. Publisher in Fleet Street, London. Published the *English Review*, Disraeli's *Curiosities of Literature*, etc.

MURRAY, John (2), (1778-1843), son of (1). Carried on his father's business in London. He issued the travels of Mungo Park, Belzoni, Perry, Franklin, etc.

MURRAY, John (3), (1808-92), son of (2). Issued the works of Livingstone, Darwin, Smiles, Smith's Dictionaries, etc.

MURRAY, Sir John (c.1768-1827) 8th Baronet of Clermont. Soldier and General who distinguished himself in the Middle East.

MURRAY, Sir John (1841-1914), born in Canada of Scottish descent, and educated in Edinburgh. Marine biologist and oceanographer. He was one of the naturalists who made the famous voyage in the *Challanger*.

MURRAY or MORAY, Sir Robert (1600-73) of Perthshire. One of the founders of the Royal Society. Buried in Westminster Abbey.

MURRAY, William Parry (1892-), born in the US of Scottish parents. Physician who made a special study of anemia, and with MINOT shared the Nobel Prize for Medicine in 1934.

MUTCH, James R. (1905-), educ. Aboyne and Aberdeen. Air Commodore (1954), Engineer Specialist Officer, Director of Tech. Training, Air Ministry (1956-59) (ret.) Was Senior Technical Staff Officer HQ Flying Training Command (1953-54).

MYLNE, Robert (1734-1811) of Edinburgh. Architect and engineer. Designed Blackfriars Bridge and planned the Gloucester and Berkeley Ship Canal. Elected FRS in 1767. Was surveyor of St. Paul's (1766-1811).

MYLNE, William Chadwell (1781-1863) son of Robert. Engineer, architect and surveyor. Constructed many reservoirs and bridges.

# N

NAIRN, James McLachlan (1859-1904). Scottish artist in New Zealand.

NAIRN, Kenneth (1898-) of Edinburgh. Air Vice-Marshal, Chartered Accountant, served on Air Council as Air Member, Accounts and Finance (1939-44), then Special Adviser on Finance to Minister for Air.

NAPIER, Sir Charles (1786-1860) of Merchiston Hall, nr. Falkirk. Admiral of the Fleet.

NAIRNE, (Carolina Oliphant), Baroness (1766-1845) of Gask, Perthshire. Songwriter, wrote 87 songs, at least four of which are immortal: 'Land o' the Leal', 'Caller Herrin', 'The Laird o' Cockpen' and 'The Auld Hoose'.

NAPIER, Sir Charles (1786-1860) of Merchiston Hall, nr. Falkirk. Admiral of the Fleet of the Queen of Portugal, defeated the Mignelite fleet and placed Donna Maria on the throne. He also defeated Ibrahim Pasha in Lebanon, attacked Acre and blockaded Alexandria.

NAPIER, John (1550-1617) of Merchiston Castle, nr. Edinburgh. Mathematician who invented logarithms (1614) and engineering devices.

NAPIER, Sir Mellis (1882-) of Dunbar. Was Chief Justice of Southern Australia (1942-67).

NAPIER, Macvey (1776-1846) of Glasgow. Lawyer and editor. Was the first professor of conveyancing in 1824. He edited the supplement to the 5th ed. of *Encyclopaedia Britannica* (1816-24) and the 7th ed. (1830-42).

NAPIER, Robert (1791-1876) of Dumbarton. Shipbuilder and engineer. Built the first four Cunard steamships and some of the earliest ironclad vessels. It was he that helped to make the Clyde a great shipbuilding centre. In 1840 he produced a Coffee Percolator which was the forerunner of the present day Cona-type Percolator.

NARES, Sir George Strong (1831-1915) of Aberdeen. Vice-Admiral and explorer. Commanded the 'Challanger' (1872-74) and the 'Alert Discovery' expeditions (1875-76).

NASMITH, David (1799-1839) of Glasgow. Philanthropist. Founded the City Missions in various cities in Europe and America.

NASMYTH, Alexander (1) (1758-1840) of Edinburgh. Portrait and landscape painter. Became known as the 'father of Scottish landscape painting'. Probably best remembered for his small portrait of Robert Burns, the portrait so often reproduced.

NASMYTH, James (2) (1808-90) of Edinburgh. Engineer son of (1). Invented the steam hammer in 1839 and later a pile driver and a dentist's drill.

NASMYTH, Patrick (3) (1787-1831) of Edinburgh. Son of (1). Landscape painter, sometimes called the 'English Hobbema'.

NEAGLE, Dame Anna (born Marjorie Robertson, daughter of a Scotsman). Famous actress and dancer, made 36 films. She was the first British actress to be created a Dame of the British Empire.

NEILL, Alexander Sutherland (1883-1973) of Forfar. Educationist, journalist, child psychologist and author. Produced many publications on child psychology.

NEILSON, James Beaumont (1792-1865) of Shettleston. Engineer and inventor. In 1828 he patented the technique of preheating the air in blast furnaces known as the hot blast process.

NELSON Sir Hugh Muir (1836-1906) of Kilmarnock. Premier of Queensland, Australia (1893-98).

NELSON, Thomas (1780-1861) of Stirlingshire. Publisher. The firm of Nelson which he founded was a pioneer in the use of the rotary press and of the half-tone blocks.

NICHOL, John (1) (1833-94) of Glasgow. Writer and poet. Produced books on Byron, Bacon, Burns, American literature (1882), etc.

NICHOL, John P (2) (1804-59) of Glasgow, father of (1). Astronomer who became well known for his public lectures.

NICHOLL, John (1894-) educ. Stirling and Glasgow. Professor of English language and literature in the Univ. of Birmingham, and visiting Prof. of English, Univ. of Pittsburg, USA (1963-65 and 1967-68).

NICHOLL, Sir William Robertson (1851-1923) of Lumsden. Man of Letters. Editor of *The Expositor* and the *British Weekly* (1886). Wrote books on Theory and Literature.

NICHOLSON, Peter (1765-) of Preston Kirk. Became a distinguished mathematician and architect. Compiled an Architectural dictionary.

NICHOLSON, William (1781-1844). Scottish portrait painter born in Ovingham-on-Tyne. Noted for his portraits of Sir Walter Scott and other famous contemporaries.

NICOL, Cameron Macdonald (1891-1965) of Aberdeen. Brigadier in Indian Medical Service. Director of Public Health, Punjab (1936-41).

NICOL, Erskine (1825-1904) of Leith. Artist painter of homely incidents in Irish and Scottish life.

NICOL, William (c.1768-1851). Scottish Physicist and inventor of the Nicol Prism which bears his name.

NINIAN, St Lowland Scots Ringan (c.360-430) from the shores of the Solway Firth. The first known Apostle of Scotland. Made a pilgrimage to Rome and was consecrated Bishop by the Pope.

NISBET, Stanley (1912-). Educ. Dunfermline and Edinburgh. Prof. of Education, Univ. of Glasgow (1951-). Research Officer at the Air Ministry (1944-46). Lecturer on Education, Univ. of Manchester (1946) and Prof. of Education, Queen's Univ., Belfast (1946-51).

NIVEN, David (1910-83) of Kirriemuir. Became an actor of world-wide renown.

NOBLE, Sir Peter (1899-) Scottish Principal of King's Coll., Univ. London (1952-68). Sometime Governor of St Thomas's Hospital.

# O

OGG, Sir William G. (1891-) of Cults, Aberdeenshire. Director of Rothmanstead Experimental Station (1943-58). Sometime foreign member of the All-union Academy of Agricultural Science in the USSR.

OGILBY, John (1600-76) of Edinburgh. Topographer, printer and map maker. Surveyor of the gutted sites after the Great Fire of London (1666). His more important maps and atlases included Africa (1670) and Asia (1673). His road atlas of Gt. Britain was unfinished (1675).

OGILVIE, Lady Mary, daughter of the late Prof. A. Macaulay of Glasgow. Principal of St Anne's Coll., Oxford (1953-).

OGILVY, Angus (1928-). Company Director. Married HRH Princess Alexandra of Kent. Pres., Scottish Wild Life Trust, Imperial Cancer Research Fund, Brit. Rheumatism and Arthritis Assoc., Chairman Nat. Assoc. of Youth Clubs, etc.

ORCHARDSON, Sir William Quiller (1832-1910) of Edinburgh. Painter of portraits and industrial social and historical subjects. His *Napoleon on board the Bellerophon* (1880) is in the Tate Gallery. Elected RA in 1877.

ORR, Robin (1909-) of Brechin. Composer. Professor of Music, Cambridge Univ. Fellow of St John's College (1965-).

OSWALD, Richard (1704-84) of Watten, Caithness. Appointed Plenipotentiary for Gt. Britain in 1782 and sent to Paris where he concluded a peace treaty with the USA which he cosigned with Benjamin Franklin. He then became known as 'Richard the Peacemaker'.

OWEN, Robert Dale (1801-77) of Glasgow. Went to America in 1825 to help in the New Harmony colony. Edited the *Free Inquirer* in New York, was a member of the Indiana legislature and entered Congress in 1843. Was Minister at Naples (1853-58) and an abolitionist and spiritualist.

# P

PARK, Mungo (1771-1806) of Foulshiels nr. Selkirk. Botanist and explorer in Africa, and of the River Niger. Discovered the source of the Niger in 1796. Told of his adventures in *Travels in the Interior of Africa* (1799).

PARKER, Agnes, of Irvine. Artist and wood engraver. Walter Brewster prize winner at 1st International Exhibition of engravings and lithography, Chicago, in 1929.

PATERSON, James R. K. (1897-) Scottish Professor of Radiotherapeutics at Univ. of Manchester (1960-). Director of Radiotherapy, Christie Hosp. and Holt Radium Inst. (1931-62).

PATERSON, Neil (1915-). Educ. Banff and Edinburgh. Author. Director, Grampian TV. Award winner, American Academy of Motion Picture Arts and Sciences (1960). His publications inc. *Behold Thy Daughter* (1950) and *Man on the Tight Rope* (1953).

PATERSON, Robert (1715-1801) from near Hawick. The original 'Old Mortality', for over 40 years, devoted himself to repairing and erecting headstones to Covenanting martyrs, neglecting his wife and five children.

PATERSON, William (1658-1719) of Skipmyre, Dumfriesshire. Financier. Founder of the Bank of England and one of its first Directors in 1694.

PATERSON, William J. M. (1911-). Educ. Glasgow. British Deputy High Commissioner, Madras (1961-). First Sec. Beirut (1947-50), Damascus (1950), Santiago (1951-53), Foreign Office (1953-55), Counsellor, Baghdad and Oslo (1955-61).

PATON, George P. (1882-) of Angus. Commercial Consultant at

Moscow (1930- 37), Consul-General Istanbul (1937-42), Director, Intelligence Div., Far Eastern Bureau, Brit. Min. of Information, New Delhi (1943-46).

PATON, Herbert J. (1887-1969) of Abernethy. Author and editor. Chairman, Board of the Faculty of Social Studies (1944-46), and of Bd. of Studies for Psychology (1950-52). Visiting Professor, Univ. of New York (1955).

PATON, John (-d.1684) of Fenwick, Ayrshire. Covenanter who became a Captain in the army of Gustavus Adolphus.

PATON, John Gibson (1824-1907) of Kirkmahoe, Dumfriesshire. Missionary of the Reformed Presbyterian church, New Hebrides (1858).

PATON, Sir Joseph Noel (1821-1901) of Dunfermline. Sculptor, painter and poet. RSA and Queen's Limner for Scotland from 1865. Exhibited at the Royal Academy (1856-83).

PATON, Robert Young (1894-1973) of Perth. Consulting Surgeon. Medical Supt., Mary's Hosp., Paddington (1924-27). Sometime Consulting Surgeon, Princess Louise Kensington Hosp. for children.

PATON, William C. (1886-). Educ. Glasgow and Edinburgh. Major-General. Surgeon-General, Bengal (1941-45). Was Inspector-General of Civil Hospitals, NW Frontier Province (1939-41).

PATON, William Douglas (1874-1953) of Jedburgh. Vice-Admiral with distinguished service in the Great War.

PATRICK, James M. (1907-). Educ. Dundee and Glasgow. Painter and etcher. Had paintings purchased for National Galleries, Millbank, South Africa, and Southern Australia.

PAUL, John (known as John Paul Jones) (1747-92) of Abigland, Kirkbean, Kirkcudbrightshire. Admiral and founder of the American Navy. He had also served in the French Navy and as Rear Admiral in the Russian Navy (1788-89). Was buried with honours at the US Naval Academy, Annapolis. He added 'Jones' to his name when he joined the US Navy in 1775.

PENDER, Sir John (1815-96) of Vale of Leven, Fife. Manufacturer of textiles and cables. He promoted cable enterprise in all parts of the world. Sometime represented Wick Burgh, Caithness, in Parliament.

PENNY, Jose' Campbell (1893-). Educ. Edinburgh. Became Political Adviser to British Admin. in ex-Italian colonies in Africa (1946-50), UK Representative on UN Consul for Libya (1950-51).

PENTLAND (Henry John Sinclair) 2nd Baron, of Lyth, Caithness.

Sometime Director and Vice-President of the American British Electrical Corp. (New York) and of Hunting Surveys Inc., New York.

PEPLOE, Samuel John (1871-1935) of Edinburgh. Artist whose still life paintings brought him fame as a colourist. He also painted landscapes and portraits. (RSA 1927).

PETTIE, John (1839-93) of Edinburgh. Painter. His works, apart from portraits were mainly historical and literary subjects, and had considerable popularity (RA 1873).

PHILIP, Dr John (1775-1851) of Kirkcaldy. Missionary in S. Africa. First Superintendent of the London Missionary Society.

PHILLIP, John (1817-67) of Aberdeen. Painter (RA 1859). Worked in London from 1836. His best works were in Spanish themes.

PICKEN, Andrew (1788-1833) of Paisley. Author. Published a series of novels including *The Sectarian* (1829), *The Dominie's Legacy* (1830) and *Waltham* (1833).

PICKEN, Ebenezar (1769-1816) of Paisley. Poet. Published several vols. of Scots poems and a *Pocket Dictionary of Scottish Dialect* (1818).

PINKERTON, Allan (1819-84) of Glasgow. Detective in the USA where in Chicago he established the agency which bears his name. Became head of the US Secret Service in 1861, and was prominent in many celebrated cases, including the breaking up of the 'Molly Maguires'.

PIRIE, Norman W. (1907-) of Stirlingshire. Demonstrator in the Biochemical Lab., Cambridge (1932-40). Became head of the Biochemistry Dept., Rothamstead Experimental Station, Harpenden in 1947.

PITCAIRN, Robert (1747-70). Scottish midshipman. Pitcairn Island is named after him because he was the first to have sighted it.

PITCAIRN, Robert (1793-1855) of Edinburgh. Antiquary and writer. Was editor of *Criminal Trials in Scotland 1484-1624* (1830-33).

PITCAIRN, Archibald (1652-1713) of Edinburgh. Physician and Satirist. He was the founder of the Medical Faculty of Edinburgh.

PLAYFAIR, John (1748-1819) of Benvie near Dundee. Mathematician and geologist. A strong supporter of the Huttonian theory in geology. He wrote *Elements of Geometry* (1795), *Outlines of Natural Philosophy* (1812-16) and *Illustrations of the Huttonian Theory of Earth* (1802). Elected FRS in 1807.

PLAYFAIR, William Henty (1789-1857). Born in London of Scottish parents. Architect. Designed Donaldson's Hospital, the National Monument, National Gallery and many other Edinburgh buildings.

PLENDERLEITH, Harold J. (1898-). Educ. Dundee. Was appointed Director in 1959 of the International Centre for the study of the Preservation of Cultural Property (created by UNESCO).

POLLOCK, Robert (1798-1827) of Muirhouse, Renfrewshire. Poet. His best work was 'The Course of Time' (1827) a poetical description of the spiritual life of man.

POLSON, William of Paisley. About 1840 with John Brown produced a cornflour powder when they were trying to make starch for cloth from maize. Later Brown and Polson became part of a worldwide concern, marketing a large range of other food products.

PONT, Timothy (c.1560-1630), educ. St Andrews. Geographer, mathematician, cartographer and Minister of Dunnet, Caithness (1601). Produced the first Scottish Atlas.

PORTEOUS, Alexander (1896-) of Haddington. Professor of Education, Univ. of Liverpool (1954-63). Prof. of Philosophy at South Coll. Northampton, Mass. USA (1926-30) and at McGill Univ. Montreal (1930-32).

PORTEOUS, Revd Norman (1898-) of Haddington. Professor of Hebrew and Semetic Languages, Univ. of Edinburgh (1937-). Principal of New Coll. and Dean of the Faculty of Divinity, Edinburgh (1964-).

PRINGLE, Sir John (1707-82) of Stichill, Roxburghshire. Founder of modern military medicine. Appointed Physician-General to the forces in the Low Countries in 1744. (FRS 1752). His *Observations on the Diseases of the Army* (1752) laid down principles of military sanitation and ventilation of barracks, hospitals and ships. He did much to improve the conditions of servicemen.

PRINGLE, Thomas (1789-1834) of Blaiklaw, Roxburghshire. Writer who for three years was Govt. Librarian at Capetown. On his return to London he became Sec. to the Anti-slavery Society in 1826.

# R

RAE, Dr John (1813-93) of Stromness, Orkney. Explorer and Arctic traveller. Commanded an expedition (1853-54) to King William's Land. In 1854 he discovered the fate of the Franklin expedition, for which he was awarded £10,000. In 1860 he surveyed a telegraph line to America via Faroes and Iceland, and in 1864 surveyed a telegraph line from Winnipeg over the Rocky mountains. He also mapped the north coast of Canada for the Hudson's Bay Co.

RAE, Sir Robert (1894-). Director of the National Agricultural Advisory Service (1948-59). Agricultural Attaché, British Embassy, Washington (1944-45).

RAEBURN, Sir Henry (1756-1823) of Stockbridge, near Edinburgh. Famous artist and portrait painter (RA 1815). Sometimes called the 'Scottish Reynolds'.

RAEBURN, John (1833-1909) of Fife. Violin maker, painter, astronomer and poet.

RAINY, Robert (1826-1906). Scottish divine who carried the union (1900) of the Free and United Presbyterian Church as the United Free Church, of which he became the Moderator.

RAIT, Sir Robert Sangster (1874-1945). Born in Leicestershire of Scots parents. Historian who was Historiographer-Royal for Scotland (1919-29).

RAMSAY, Sir Alexander (-d.1332). Scottish patriot famed for his deeds of bravery. He was captured and starved to death at Hermitage Castle by William Douglas 'The Flower of Chivalry'.

RAMSAY, Allan (1685-1759) of Leadhills, Lanarkshire. Pastoral poet. *The Gentle Shepherd*, a pastoral comedy, (1725) and *Thirty Fables*

(1730) his most popular. Was by trade a wigmaker. He created the first circulating library in Gt. Britain, and was also noted for his efforts to establish a theatre in Edinburgh.

RAMSAY, Allan (1713-84), son of Ramsay of Leadhills. Portrait painter of distinction. Had great success in London.

RAMSAY, Sir Andrew Crombie (1814-91) of Glasgow. Geologist. Appointed Director-General of the Geological Survey in 1871. He was the first to mention the glacial origin of 'Drift'. Elected FRS in 1863.

RAMSAY, Andrew Michael (1686-1743) of Ayr. Theologian and writer.

RAMSAY, Edward Bannerman Burnett (1793-1872) of Aberdeen. Divine and writer of various religious works. His *Reminiscences of Scottish Life and Character* (1857) was delightful.

RAMSAY, Sir William (1852-1916) of Glasgow. Professor of Chemistry at Bristol (1880-87) and Univ. Coll., London (1887-1912). In conjunction with Lord Rayleigh he discovered the gas Argon in 1894. Later he discovered Helium, Neon, Krypton and Xenon, and won a Nobel Prize for Chemistry in 1904. Elected FRS in 1888.

RANDOLPH, Sir Thomas, 1st Earl of Moray (-d.1332). Soldier and statesman and comrade of Bruce who created him Earl of Moray. He commanded a division at Bannockburn, took Berwick (1318), won the victory of Mitton (1319), re-invaded England (1320 and 1327), and was Regent from Bruce's death (1329) until his own.

RANKIN, Henry C. D. (1888-1965) of Ayrshire. Surgeon and Major-General. Served with distinction in the 1914-18 War. Surgeon to C in C India (1923-25) and (1927-31), Surgeon to the Governor, Bombay (1936-37). Deputy Director Medical Services in India Commands (1941-46).

RANKIN, Robert (1915-), educ. Fettes and Cambridge. Professor of Mathematics, Glasgow Univ. (1954-). Prof. of Pure Mathematics at Birmingham Univ. (1951-54). Visiting Professor, Indiana Univ. (1963-64).

RANKINE, William John Macquorn (1820-72) of Edinburgh. Engineer and physicist. His work on the steam engine, machinery, shipbuilding, applied mechanics, metal fatigue, etc., became standard textbooks. He it was who evolved the scientific term 'Energy'. Considered to be the founder of the science of thermodynamics. Elected FRS in 1853.

REDPATH, Anne (1895-1965) of Galashields. Artist. Her oil and watercolour paintings showed great richness of colour. One of the most

important modern Scottish artists. Elected RSA in 1952.
REID, Sir Alexander (1889-1968), educ. Glasgow and Australia. Member of the Commonwealth Grants Commission (1954-). Under-Treasurer, Govt. of West Australia (1938-54).
REID, Archibald C. (1915-), educ. Edinburgh and Cambridge. Secretary for Fijian Affairs (1959-). Was British Agent and Consul in Tonga (1957).
REID, Sir Francis (1900-1970) of Bearsden. Brigadier (1950), Commander, Ceylon Garrison and UK troops in Ceylon (1949-50), Cyprus District (1950-51), Cyrenacia District (1951-52) and Ceylon Army (1952-55).
REID, Sir George (1841-1912) of Aberdeen. Painter of portraits and landscapes. President of the Royal Scottish Academy (1891-1902). Elected RSA in 1877.
REID, Sir George Houston (1845-1918) of Johnston, Renfrew. Politician and statesman. Premier of New South Wales (1894-99) and Prime Minister of Australia (1904-05).
REID, James Scott Cunningham, Baron (life peer) of Drem (1890-) of East Lothian. Lord of Appeal in Ordinary (1948-). Solicitor-General for Scotland (1936-41), Lord Advocate (1941-45), Dean of the Faculty of Advocates (1945-48). Chairman, Malaya Constitutional Commission (1956-57).
REID, John (1906-) of Callander. Chief Veterinary Officer, Ministry of Agriculture, Fisheries and Food (1965-).
REID or Robertson, John (1721-1807) of Perthshire. Soldier and musician. Entered the army in 1745 and rose to the rank of General. He was a flute player and composer.
REID, Louis A. (1895-) of Ellon. Professor of Philosophy of Education, Inst. of Education, London Univ. (1947-62).
REID, Thomas (1710-96) of Strachan Manse. Eminent Philosopher. Wrote several books on metaphysical subjects including an essay on 'The Intellectual Powers of Man' (1785) and 'Actual Powers of the Human Mind' (1788).
REID, Sir Thomas Wemyss (1842-1905). Scottish journalist and biographer born at Newcastle upon Tyne. Editor of the *Speaker* (1890-99). He wrote *Lives of Charlotte Bronte* and *Lord Houghton* and several novels.
REID, Sir William (1791-1858) of Kingussie. Meteorologist, soldier and administrator. Served with distinction in the Peninsular War, and

was Governor of Bermuda, Windward Islands and Malta.

REITH, John Charles Welsham, 1st Baron of Stonehaven (1889-1971). Administrator who became known as the 'Father of the BBC' (1927-38), Minister of Information (1940), Min. of Transport (1940), Min. of Works and Building (1940-42). First Chairman of BOAC (1939-40). Director of Combined Operations Material at Admiralty (1943-45).

RENNIE, George (1) (1791-1866) born in London son of John (3). Engineer with his brother John (4) carried on an immense business of shipbuilding, railways, bridges, harbours, docks, machinery and marine engines. Sometime Superintendent of the machinery of the Royal Mint.

RENNIE, (2) Sir Gilbert (1895-), educ. Stirling and Glasgow. Governor and C in C, Northern Rhodesia (1948-54). High Commissioner in UK for the Federation of Rhodesia and Nyasaland (1954-61).

RENNIE, (3) John (1761-1821) of Phantassie Farm, East Linton. Civil engineer. Builder of bridges, canals and docks. Built some 60 bridges including Waterloo and Southwark. He built the London and East and West India Docks, and docks at Leith, Plymouth, Liverpool, Dublin, Hull, Chatham and Portsmouth. The Kennet and Avon Canal was also his work.

RENNIE, (4) Sir John (1794-1874) son of John (3) and brother of George (1). Engineer. Was knighted on his completion of the construction of London Bridge in 1831.

RENWICK, William L. (1889-1970) of Glasgow. Professor of Rhetoric and English Literature, Univ. of Edinburgh (1945-49). Prof. of English Language and Literature, King's Coll., Newcastle upon Tyne and in the Univ. of Durham (1921-45). Visiting Prof. to China (1943-44).

RICHARDSON, Frank M. (1904-), educ. Glenalmond and Edinburgh. Physician. Major-General (1957). Director of Medical Services, BAOR (1956-61).

RICHARDSON, Sir John (1787-1865) of Dumfries. Naturalist, physician and Arctic explorer. Commanded the expedition in search of Franklin (1848-49).

RIDDELL, Henry Scott (-d.1870) of Teviothead. Songwriter and minister. 'Scotland Yet' and 'Oor Ain Folk' are from his pen.

RILEY, James, of Glasgow. Engineer who discoverd nickel steel in 1889.

RITCHIE, Andrew E. (1915-), educ. Edinburgh and Aberdeen.

Professor of Physiology, United Coll. of Univ. of St Andrews (1958-). Scientific Adviser, Civil Defence (1961-).

RITCHIE, Sir Douglas (1885-) of Aberdeenshire. Became Chief Executive of London Port Emergency Committee (1939-46).

RITCHIE, Sir John (1904-) educ. Turiff and Edinburgh. Became Principal and Dean of the Royal Veterinary Coll., Univ. of London in 1965.

RITCHIE, John K., 3rd Baron Ritchie of Dundee (1902-). Was Chairman of the Stock Exchange from 1959 till 1965.

RITCHIE, Kenneth Gordon (1921-) of Arbroath. Was appointed High Commissioner in Guyana in 1967.

RITCHIE, William (1781-1831) of Fifeshire. Solicitor and writer. One of the founders of the *Scotsman* (1816).

RITCHIE-CALDER, Peter R., Baron (life peer) (1906-) of Forfar. Author, Scientific Social and Political journalist and broadcaster. Director of Plans of Political Warfare in the Foreign Office (1941-45). Chairman, Metrication Bd. (1969-). Fellow of the World Academy of Arts and Science. Has written over 30 books which have been translated into more than 40 languages.

ROB ROY, (Robert Macgregor) (1671-1734) of Glen Gyle, Perthshire. Notorious freebooter. Helped the poor at the expense of the rich.

ROBB, Andrew McCance (1887-1968), educ. Glasgow. Professor of Naval Architecture in Univ. of Glasgow (1944-57). Practised as a consulting Naval architect, (1925-44).

ROBERTSON, Sir Hugh (1874-1952) of Glasgow. Conductor of the Glasgow Orpheus Choir, which achieved international renown.

ROBERTS, David (1796-1864) of Edinburgh. Painter. Among his pictures were *Departure of the Israelites from Egypt* (1829), *Jerusalem* (1845), *Rome* (1853) and *Grand Canal of Venice* (1856). RA 1841.

ROBERTSON, Archibald (1853-) of Edinburgh. Divine. Bishop of Exeter (1903-16). Appointed Principal of King's College in 1897.

ROBERTSON, Fyfe (1902-87) of Edinburgh. Journalist and TV personality. Was picture editor of the *Picture Post* until it ceased publication.

ROBERTSON, George Croom (1842-92) of Aberdeen. Philosopher. In 1866 became Professor of Mental Philosophy and Logic at Univ. Coll., London.

ROBERTSON of Brackla (Ian Argyll). Major-General. Brigade Major, 152 Bde. 51st (H) Div. (1943), Commanded 51st (H) Div.

(1964-66), Director of Army Equipment, MOD (1966-68).

ROBERTSON, James Logie (1846-1922) of Milnathort. Poet who feigned to be a shepherd 'Hugh Haliberton'. His works incl. 'Horace Homespun' (1886) and 'Ochil Idylls' (1891).

ROBERTSON, James (c.1720-88) of Fifeshire. Soldier who became Governor of New York in 1779, and Commander in Chief, Virginia in 1780.

ROBERTSON, Sir James (1899-) of Broughty Ferry. Governor-General and C in C of the Federation of Nigeria (1955-60). Director of Uganda Co. (1961-), and other high offices in East Africa.

ROBERTSON, James, of Paisley. A grocer who founded what is now one of the largest preserve manufacturers in the world.

ROBERTSON, James C. (1813-82) of Aberdeen. Divine and author of the *History of the Christian Church*. Was appointed Canon of Canterbury in 1859.

ROBERTSON, John M. (1900-) of Auchterarder. Professor of Chemistry, Univ. of Glasgow (1942-). Director of Laboratories (1955-). Visiting Professor, Univ. of California, Berkeley, USA (1958). President, Chemical Soc. (1962-64).

ROBERTSON, John Mackinnon (1856-1933) of Arran. Politician, critic and editor of the *National Observer* in London (1891-93). Was Liberal MP for Tyneside and rose to be Secretary to the Board of Trade and Privy Counsellor.

ROBERTSON, Joseph (1810-66) of Aberdeen. Antiquary who contributed much to *Chamber's Encyclopaedia*.

ROBERTSON, Sir MacPherson (1860-1945). Born of Scottish parents at Ballarat, Australia. Founder of the Australian confectionary firm that bears his name. He gave a large sum of money towards the expenses of the Australian Antarctic Expedition (1929-30). MacRobertson Land in Antarctica commemorates his name. It was Robertson who initiated the air race from England to Australia.

ROBERTSON, William (1721-93) of Borthwick, Midlothian. Minister and historian. His *History of Scotland 1542-1603* (1759) was a great success, and was followed by his *History of the Reign of the Emperor Charles V* (1769), his most valuable work for which he received £4,500 and high praise from Voltaire and Gibbon.

ROBERTSON, Sir William (1860-1933). Scottish soldier believed to be the only British soldier to rise from private to Field-Marshal, (CIGS 1915-18).

RODGER, Thomas R. (1878-1968). Educ. Lanark, Glasgow and Edinburgh. Aural surgeon. Senior surgeon, Ear Nose and Throat Dept., Hull Royal Infirmary (1919-38). Group Officer, Min. of Health (1939-46).

ROLLOCK, Robert (c.1555-99) of Powis, nr. Stirling. Became first Principal of Edinburgh Univ. in 1583. He wrote *Latin Commentaries.*

ROPER, Andrew, of Hawick. A farmer who in 1737 invented the winnowing machine.

ROSEBERRY, (6th Earl of Roseberry) (1882-1974) of Balmeny, Edinburgh. Great sporting personality, sometimes called 'The Grand Old Man of Racing'.

ROSS, Alexander (1880-) of Forres. Barrister and Brigadier-General. Judge of District Court of Yorkton, Saskatchewan (1921-55).

ROSS, Alexander David (1883-1966) of Glasgow. Executive Officer, Pan-Indian Ocean Science Assoc. East-West Centre, Univ. of Hawaii, Honolulu (1961-64).

ROSS, Sir David (1877-) of Thurso, Caithness. Appointed Chairman Civil Service Tribunal (1942-52) & Royal Commission on the Press (1947-49). Hon. Fellow of Merton, Balliol and Oriel Coll., and of Trinity Coll., Dublin.

ROSS, Frank M. (1891-) of Glasgow. Chairman, Canadian Executive Committee and joint Chief Executive, Lafarge Canada Co. Ltd. Sometime Director-General of Production of Naval Armaments and Equipment, Dept. of Munitions and Supply, Canada.

ROSS, Sir Hew D. (1779-1868) of Galloway. Soldier and Field-Marshal who served with distinction under Wellington.

ROSS, James (1848-1913) of Cromarty. Civil Engineer. Constructed rlys. in the US and Canada. Built the mountain sections of the Canadian Pacific Rly. (1883-85). Financed and built, with others, tramway systems in Montreal, Toronto, England, West Indies and Mexico.

ROSS, Sir James Clark (1800-62) born in London of Wigtownshire forebears. Rear-Admiral and explorer. Discovered the Ross Sea which bears his name. He was also responsible, with his uncle Sir John Ross for the establishment of the true position of the magnetic north.

ROSS, John born near Lookout Mountain, Tennessee in 1790, son of a Scottish emigrant. Became a Cherokee Indian Chief.

ROSS, Sir John (1777-1856) of Wigtownshire. Rear-Admiral and explorer in Baffin Bay. Discovered the Boothia Peninsula in his search for the north-west passage to the pole. With his nephew Sir James Clark Ross he established the true position of magnetic north. Was Consul at Stockholm (1839-46).

ROSS, Sir John Lockhart (1721-90) of Lanarkshire. Vice-Admiral, with distinguished service in the Channel and North Sea.

ROSS, Sir Ronald (1857-1932) born in Almora, India of Scots descent. Made the discovery (1895-98) that malaria parasites were carried by mosquitos and transmitted to their victims while sucking blood.

ROSS, Sir William Charles (1794-1860). Painter. Painted many portraits of the Royal Family. Appointed miniature painter to the Queen in 1837.

ROW (1) John (c.1525-80), educ. at Stirling and St Andrews. Scottish reformer. Was four times Moderator of the General Assembly.

ROW (2) John (1568-1646), eldest son of (1). Minister. Wrote a prolix but reliable *History of the Kirk of Scotland*. He was strongly opposed to the introduction of Episcopacy into Scotland.

ROXBURGH, William, of Ayrshire. Botanist. Appointed Superintendent of Calcutta Botanical Gardens in 1793. Wrote *The Standard Flora of India*. Became known as the 'Father of Indian Botany'.

ROY, William (1726-99) of Miltonhead, Lanarkshire. Surveyor and soldier. Prepared the 'Great Map' of Scotland. Appointed Major-General and Military Surveyor in 1781. Regarded by many as the father of Ordnance Survey. Elected FRS in 1767.

RUDDIMAN, Thomas (1674-1757), of Boyndie, Banffshire. Classical grammarian and philologist. Editor of Latin works.

RUNCIE, Dr Alexander Kennedy, born at Liverpool in 1921, son of a Scottish electrical engineer from Kilmarnock. Enthroned Archbishop of Canterbury, March 1980. He was a wartime Scots Guards Officer and holder of the MC.

RUSSEL, Alexander (1814-76) of Edinburgh. Journalist and editor of the *Scotsman* from 1848. An antagonist of the Corn Laws.

RUSSELL, John Scott (1808-82) of Parkhead, Glasgow. Civil and Naval Architect and engineer. Inventor of the 'Wave system' of shipbuilding. He built the *Great Eastern* and many other ships.

RUTHERFORD, Charles (1858-1922) of Edinburgh. Veterinary surgeon. Became Principal Veterinary Officer, India in 1908, a position he held till 1913.

RUTHERFORD, Daniel (1749-1819) of Edinburgh. Physician and botanist. In 1772 published his discovery of the distinction between 'noxious air' (nitrogen) and carbon dioxide. Subsequent study on the constitution of natural gases was founded on his work. He was the inventor of a max.-min. thermometer in 1794.

RUTHERFORD, Ernest Lord Rutherford of Nelson (1871-1937), New Zealand born of Scots descent. 4th son of 12 children. Physicist and pioneer in atomic research. The first to split the atom.

RUTHERFORD, John G. (1857-1923) of Peebleshire. Veterinary surgeon. Veterinary Director-General (1902-12) and Live Stock Commissioner (1906-1912) for Canada. Sometime Commissioner, Board of Rly. Comm. for Canada.

RUTHERFORD, Samuel (1600-61) of Nisbet, near Jedburgh. Theologian and preacher. Prof. of Divinity at St Andrews (1639) and Principal (1647). His chief fame rested upon his devotional works, such as *Christ dying and drawing sinners to himself* (1649).

# S

SCOT, Sir John (1585-1670) of Cupar. Pioneer map maker and scholar.

SCOT, Michael (c.1175-1234) of Balwearie. Scholar and mathematician attached to the Court of the Holy Roman Emperor Frederick II. He wrote works on astrology, astronomy and alchemy and became popular as a magician and sometimes known as the 'Wonderous Wizard'.

SCOTT, Alastair Ian (1928-), educ. Glasgow. Professor of Chemistry, Texas A & M Univ. (1977-). Prof. Univ. of Columbia (1962-65), Univ. of Sussex (1965-68) and Yale Univ. (1968-77). Elected FRS 1978.

SCOTT, Alexander (c.1525-84) from near Edinburgh. Lyrical poet.

SCOTT, Alexander Whiteford (1904-) of Glasgow. Professor of Chemical Engineering, Univ. of Strathclyde, Glasgow (1955-71). Was Hon. Engineering Consultant to the Min. of Agri., Fisheries and Food (1946-62).

SCOTT, David (1806-49) of Edinburgh. Historical painter. His painting *The Vintager* is in the National Gallery. RSA (1829).

SCOTT, Duncan Campbell (1862-1947) born in Canada, son of a Scottish missionary. Poet and writer of short stories. Known chiefly as Canada's Poet Laureate. His pieces 'The Forsaken' and 'Half-breed Girl' are among the most famous in Canadian poetry.

SCOTT, Francis George (1880-1958) of Hawick. Composer described as probably the most original and substantial composer Scotland has yet produced. His works include the orchestral suite *The Seven Deadly Sins*.

SCOTT, Sir Ian Dixon (1909-) of Inverness. Diplomat. First Sec. Foreign Office (1950-51), Brit. Legation Helsinki (1952), Brit.

Embassy, Beirut (1954-59), Consul-General then Ambassador to the Congo (1960-61), to Sweden (1961-65) and Norway (1965-68).

SCOTT, John (1784-1821) of Aberdeen. Journalist, author and critic. Became first editor of the *London Magazine* in 1820. He was mortally wounded in a duel in London.

SCOTT, Michael (1789-1835) of Glasgow. Businessman and author. Spent some time in the West Indies. His *Tom Cringle's Log* (1829-33) and *The Cruise of the Midge* (1834-35) considered among his best works.

SCOTT, Paul Henderson (1920-) of Edinburgh. Consul-General, Vienna (1968-) and Milan (1977-).

SCOTT, Sir Robert (1905-) of Peterhead. Minister, Brit. Embassy, Washington (1953-55). Commissioner-General for UK in SE Asia (1955-59). Permanent Sec. Min. of Defence (1961-63).

SCOTT, Thomas (1897-1968) of Montrose. Major-General. Chief of Staff to C in C Ceylon (1944), Director of Manpower, Planning GHQ India (1944-46) and Deputy Chief of General Staff (B) GHQ, India (1946-47).

SCOTT, Sir Walter (1771-1832) of Edinburgh. Novelist, historian, poet, antiquarian and sheriff. Prolific writer with famous works too numerous to mention here.

SCOTT, William Bell (1811-90) of Edinburgh. Painter, illustrator and poet.

SCOTT, William (1913-) of Greenock. Painter–predominately abstract. His work is noted for its sensitive handling and colour.

SCOTT-ELLIOT, James (1902-) of Dumfriesshire? Major-General (1954). GOC 51st (H) Division (1952-56).

SCOTT-MONCRIEFF, Sir Colin Campbell (1836-1916). Scottish engineer and administrator. Played a great part in Egyptian irrigation.

SEATH, Thomas Bollen (1820-1903) of Prestonpans. Shipbuilder and designer of steam yachts, ferry vessels, hopper barges, etc.

SELKIRK, Alexander (1676-1721) of Largo, Fife. Seafarer, whose story of his time on Juan Fernandez island where he lived alone for four years and four months, is supposed to have suggested the *Robinson Crusoe* of Defoe.

SELKIRK, Thomas Douglas, 5th Earl of (1771-1820). Explorer and colonizer. Settled emigrants from the Scottish Highlands in Prince Edward Island (1803) and Red River Valley, Manitoba. Became known as 'Selkirk of Red River'.

SELLAR, William Young (1825-90) from near Golspie. Classical scholar. He made his name widely known by his brilliant *Roman Poets of the Republic* (1863) and *The Roman Poets of the Augustan Age–Virgil* (1877).

SEMPILL, (1) Francis (c.1616-82) of Renfrewshire, son of (3). Poet and author of *The Banishment of Povertie.*

SEMPILL (2) Robert (c.1530-95) of Renfrewshire. Author of satirical and witty ballads such as 'The Legend of a Lymaris Life' and 'Siege of the Castle of Edinburgh'. He wrote coarsely satirical poems of life in his time.

SEMPILL (3) Robert (c.1595-1665) of Renfrewshire. Royalist and poet. Remembered perhaps for his ballad on the 'Life and Death of Habbie Simson, piper of Kibarchan' (1640).

SEMPILL, William F. Forbes-Sempill, 19th Baron (1893-1965). Representative Peer of Scotland (1935-68). Royal Aeronautical Society Chairman (1926-27) and President (1927-30). Competed in the King's Cup Air Race, 1924, '25, '26, '27, '28, '29 and '30.

SERVICE, Robert. Scottish bank clerk. Went to Canada to be a cowboy. Became Canada's most popular poet at the end of the nineteenth century. His first book of verse *Songs of a Sourdough* made him a fortune. 'Dangerous Dan Macgrew' was his creation too.

SHAIRP, John Campbell (1819-85) of Houston House, West Lothian. Poet. Professor of Poetry at Oxford (1877-82).

SHAND, James (Jimmy) (1908-) of East Wemyss, Fife. World famous Scottish dance band leader. An entertainer described as having magic in his fingertips on the accordion.

SHANKLY, Bill ('Shanks') (1914-81) of Ayrshire. Footballer and football club manager extraordinary. Managed Liverpool FC (1959-74). One of the all-time greats of football.

SHARP, William (1855-1905) of Paisley. Novelist, art critic and poet. Settled in London in 1879. Published *Earth's Vices* in 1884 and wrote on contemporary English, French and German poets. Under the pseudonym 'Fiona Macleod' he wrote some fine romances incl. *The Mountain Lovers* and *The Sin Eater* (1895) and later *The Immortal Hour.*

SHARPE, Charles Kirkpatrick (1781-1851) of Dumfries. Antiquarian. Contributed two original ballads to Scott's *Minstrelsy.*

SHAW, Sir James (1764-1843) of Riccarton, Ayrshire. Was Lord Mayor of London in 1805.

SHAW, Richard Norman (1831-1912) of Edinburgh. Architect who had great influence on late nineteenth century architecture.

SHEARER, Sir James G. (1893-1966) of Dundee. Was President of the Supreme Court, Asmara, Eritrea, (1953-62).

SHEARER, Moira, of Dunfermline. Actress and ballet dancer. Best remembered for her part as ballerina in the film *The Red Shoes* (1948).

SHEPHERD, Revd Robert H.W. (1888-) Educ. St Andrews and Edinburgh. Missionary of the UF Church of Scotland to S.Africa (1918), Cape Province (1920-26), Lovedale Missionary Institution (1927-58) and President of the Christian Council of South Africa (1956-60).

SHIELDS, Dr Alexander of Glasgow. Invented an improved pulsating vacuum milking machine in 1895.

SHIRREFF, Patrick (1791-1876) from near Haddington, East Lothian. Farmer who was a pioneer of cereal hybridizing and produced many varieties of wheat and oats.

SIBBALD, Sir Robert (1641-1722) of Edinburgh. Naturalist and physician. Spent much time on botany and zoology. Was virtual founder of the Royal College of Physicians, Edinburgh and became Scottish Geographer Royal.

SIM, Alastair (1900-1976) of Edinburgh. Actor and producer. Played leading roles in many popular films and on TV. His best screen performances incl. *Waterloo Road, The Happiest Days of Your Life, Green for Danger, Laughter in Paradise* and *The Belles of St Trinians.*

SIMMONDS, Keith Willison (1912-) of Lanarkshire. Diplomat and Artist. Financial Sec. Nyasaland (1951-57) and Chief Secretary Aden (1957-63). Exhibited a number of paintings in several academies.

SIMSON, Robert (1687-1764) of Kirktonhall, Ayrshire. Mathematician. His great work was his restoration of Euclid's lost treatise on Porisms (1776). His publication *The Elements of Euclid* (1756) was for a long time the standard text of Euclid in Britain.

SIMPSON, Alfred H. (Mr Justice Simpson) (1914-) of Dundee. Appointed Puisne Judge, High Court of Kenya in 1967.

SIMPSON, William (Bill) (1931-) of Ayr. Actor. Became popular as Dr Finlay in the BBC TV and Radio series *Dr Finlay's Casebook.*

SIMPSON, Sir George (1792-1860) Scottish Canadian explorer and administrator (1821-56) of Hudson's Bay Co. and its territory. Made an overland journey around the world in 1828. Simpson's Falls and Cape George Simpson are named after him.

SIMPSON, Sir James (1792-1868) of Roxburghshire. Soldier and General who served with distinction under Wellington.

SIMPSON, Sir James F. (1874-1967), educ. Falkirk and Glasgow. Chairman, Chamber of Commerce, Madras (1920-22). Sometime Governor of the Imperial Bank of India, and Consul for Norway at Madras.

SIMPSON, James. A Scotsman who in 1829 installed the first known water purification system–a method of slow filteration on sand beds.

SIMPSON, Sir James Young (1811-70) of Bathgate. Obstetrician and Professor of Midwifery. Discovered Chloroform in 1847, having experimented on himself. Surgeon to the Queen in Scotland (1847).

SIMPSON, Thomas (1808-40) of Dingwall. Explorer in the Canadian Arctic. Simpson Strait bears his name.

SIMPSON, William (1823-99) of Glasgow. Became the first war-artist correspondent during the Crimean war. Was known as 'Crimean Simpson', and was regarded as one of the most famous artist-correspondents in history.

SIMPSON, William Douglas (1896-1968) of Aberdeen. Librarian and archaeologist. Directed excavations at many old castles between 1919 and 1935 including Kildrummy, Kindrochit, Esslemont and Finavon.

SINCLAIR, Allan F. W. (1900-) of Edinburgh. Journalist and publicist. Editor of the *Sunday Graphic* (1831-36) and *Daily Sketch* (1936-39). Sometime Director, British Information Services, Middle East. Specialist Radio Photographic Adviser, India and Ceylon (1945). Joined the *Daily Herald* in 1946 and later the *Sun*.

SINCLAIR, Sir Archibald Henry MacDonald, 1st Viscount Thurso of Ulbster (1890-1970) Leader of the Liberal Party (1935-45), Sec. of State for Air in the Churchill Administration (1940-45).

SINCLAIR, Daniel (Dane) (1852-1930) of Thrumster, Caithness. Telephone engineer and inventor of the automatic telephone exchange. He was also the inventor of the hollow tube solder containing fluxite. He was regarded as one of the leading telephone engineers of his day.

SINCLAIR, Hugh Macdonald (1910-) of Edinburgh. Fellow and lecturer in Physiology and Biochemistry, Magdalen Coll., Oxford (1937-). Produced many publications on nutrition and metabolism. Director, International Institute of Human Nutrition (1972-).

SINCLAIR, James, 14th Earl of Caithness (1824-81). Patented many ingenious inventions, including a loom, steam carriage and gravitating compass.

SINCLAIR, John (Lord Pentland) 1st Baron (1866-1925) of Edinburgh. Governor of Madras (1912-19). Secretary for Scotland (1905-12).

SINCLAIR, Sir John of Ulbster (1754-1835) of Thurso. Politician and agriculturist. Founded the Board of Agriculture in 1793. Compiled the *First Statistical Account of Scotland* (1791-99). Was undoubtedly one of the most energetic and enterprising Scotsman who has ever lived.

SINCLAIR, Patrick (1736-1820) of Lybster, Caithness. General and soldier of fortune. Served with distinction in many campaigns in North America.

SINCLAIR, Robert J., 1st Baron of Cleeve (1893-) educ. Glasgow and Oxford. President, Imperial Tobacco Co. Ltd. (1959-), (Chairman 1947-59). Director-General of Army Requirements, War Office (1939-42).

SKENE, William Forbes (1809-92) of Inverie, Knoydart. Historian and biographer. His chief works, *The Highlanders of Scotland, their Origin, History and Antiquities* (1837), and *Celtic Scotland, a History of Ancient Alban* (1876-80). He was a close friend of Scott. Became Scottish Historiographer Royal in 1881.

SKINNER, James Scott (1843-1927) of Banchory. Violinist, known as the 'Strathspey king'.

SKINNER, John (1721-1807) of Birse, Aberdeenshire. Historian and songwriter. Wrote the *Ecclesiastical History of Scotland* (1788) and several songs of which 'The Ewie wi' the Crookit Horn' and 'Tullochgorum' were the best known.

SLESSOR, Mary (1849-1915) of Dundee. Missionary in Calabar, Africa for many years.

SLOAN, Sir Tennant, (1884-) of Glasgow. Was Joint Sec. Home Dept., Govt. of India (1932-36). Adviser to the Governor, United Provinces (1939-45).

SMALL, James of Berwickshire. Carpenter and ploughwright. Produced an improved swing plough in 1765 to replace the old Scotch plough of Jas. Anderson of Hermiston. It was the first attempt to design a plough on a scientific basis. He did not patent his plough, and died a poor man.

SMEATON, John (1724-92), born near Leeds, a descendant of an old Perthshire family named Smeton. Civil engineer, builder of bridges, canals and lighthouses. His Eddystone light revolutionised lighthouse design.

SMELLIE, William (1697-1763) of Lanark. Obstetrician. He laid down safe rules on the use of forceps and introduced several types.

SMELLIE, William (1740-95) of Edinburgh. Scientist and printer. One of his first great literary undertakings was the first edition of the *Encyclopaedia Britannica*–entirely planned and compiled by himself.

SMILES, Samuel (1812-1904) of Haddington. Author, social reformer and physician. Became a surgeon in Leeds and editor of the *Leeds Times*, and in 1854, Secretary of the SE Railway.

SMITH, Adam (1723-90) of Kirkcaldy. Political economist and philosopher. Wrote *The Wealth of Nations* in 1776. Regarded as the 'father' of the science of Political Economy.

SMITH, Alexander (1829-67) of Kilmarnock. Poet, novelist and pattern designer. His first and very popular publication *A Life Drama* (1853) was followed by *City Poems* (1857) and *Edwin of Deira* (1861)

SMITH, Sir George (1856-1942) Calcutta-born Scot. Biblical scholar and minister. Chaplain to the King (1933-42). His writings include *Historical Geography of the Holy Land* (1894), *The Twelve Prophets* (1896-1897), *Jerusalem* (1907) and *The Early Poetry of Israel* (1912).

SMITH, Iain Crichton, born 1928 in Lewis. Poet and novelist in English and Gaelic. His novels incl. *Consider the Lilies* (1968) and *The Last Summer* (1969)

SMITH, James (1789-1850) of Deanston, Perthshire. Agricultural Engineer and Philanthropist. The inventor of 'Thorough Drainage' by means of a subsoil plough (1823). He had also been the inventor of a rotary reaping machine in 1811.

SMITH, James D. M. (1895-1969) educ. Aberdeen. Financial Sec. Singapore (1947-51), UN Tech. Asst. Administrator, Nicaragua (1953-55), Brazil (1957-58) and Venezuela (1959-61).

SMITH, Norman Kemp (1872-1958) of Dundee. Philosopher and Professor of Psychology (1906) and of Philosophy (1914) at Princeton, USA. Was notable for his remarkable *Studies* (1902), *New Studies* (1952) and selected translations of Descartes philosophical writings (1953).

SMITH, Robert A. (1909-) of Kelso. Professor of Physics, Sheffield Univ. (1961-62). First Director, Centre of Materials Science and Engineering, Mass. Inst. of Technology (1962-69).

SMITH, Sydney Goodsir (1915-75) Scottish poet and critic born in Wellington, New Zealand. His main themes are love and nationalism. Poems incl. 'So Late into the Night' (1952), 'Figs and Thistles' (1959), 'Cokkels' (1954) and 'Under the Elder Tree' (1948).

SMITH, Walter Chalmers (1842-1908) of Aberdeen. Poet who attained a considerable reputation. He was also a minister of the Free Church of Scotland. His works included 'The Bishop's Walk' (1861) and 'A Heretic' (1890).

SMITH, Sir William Alexander (1854-1914) of Pennyland, Thurso. Founder in 1883 of the Boy's Brigade.

SMITH, William Robertson (1846-94) of Keig, Aberdeenshire. Theologian and Orientalist. In 1883 he became Lord Almoner's Prof. of Arabic at Cambridge, and in 1886 University Librarian and Adam's Prof. of Arabic in 1889. In 1887 he became chief editor of the *Encyclopaedia Britannica*.

SMOLLET, Tobias George (1721-71) of Cardross, Dunbartonshire. Novelist and surgeon. Sailed as a surgeon's mate on the expedition to Carthagena (1741). Practised in London as a surgeon. His literary work had mixed reception, and he was nicknamed 'Smelfungus' by Sterne.

SNELL, John (1629-79) of Ayrshire. Philanthropist. Founder of the Snell exhibition at Balliol Coll., Oxford.

SOMERVILLE, née Fairfax, Mary (1780-1872) of Jedburgh. Mathematician and scientific writer. Wrote *Celestial Mechanism* in 1830. Somerville College Oxford is named after her.

SOUTER, William (1898-1943) of Perth. Poet. His best works included 'In the times of Tyrants' (1939) and 'The Expectant Silence (1943). His collection *Seeds in the Wind* (1933) and *Poems in Scots* (1935) gave him a place in Scottish literature. He was bedridden for the last 14 years of his life from a form of paralysis.

SPALDING, John (c.1609-70) of Aberdeen. Diarist, royalist and Commissary clerk after whom was named a book club (1839-70).

SPARK, Muriel (1918-) of Edinburgh. Novelist and poet. Her works included *The Comforters* (1957), *The Prime of Jean Brodie* (1961) and *Mendelbaum* (1965).

SPENCE, Sir Basil Unwin (1907-76) born in India of Scottish parents. Professor of Architecture, Royal Academy. Designed the new Coventry Cathedral (1951) and many other outstanding architectural masterpieces.

SPENCE, James Lewis Thomas Chalmers (1874-1955) of Broughty-Ferry. Anthropologist, author, poet and editor. An authority on the mythology and customs of ancient Mexico, South America and the Middle East as well as Celtic Britain's. His *The Gods of Mexico* (1923) is a standard work.

SPOTTISWOOD, John (1565-1639) of Midcalder. Prelate and historian. Sometime Archbishop of Glasgow and St Andrews, and in 1635 Lord Chancellor of Scotland. His publications include *History of the Church of Scotland* (1635).

SPOTTISWOODE, Alicia Ann (Lady John Scott), (1810-1900) of Lauder. Poetess, composer and author. Became known for her Scottish songs 'Durisdeer' and others. She wrote 'Annie Laurie' and composed the music.

STAIR (1) James Dalrymple, 1st Viscount (1619-95) of Ayrshire. President of the Court of Session and member of the Privy Council (1670-).

STAIR (2) Sir John Dalrymple, 1st Earl of (1648-1707) son of (1) above. Judge and politician. Was Lord Advocate under William III and as Sec. of State from 1691 had chief management of Scottish affairs.

STAIR (3), John Dalrymple (1673-1747) of Edinburgh. Soldier. Was aide-de-camp to Marlborough in 1703. Distinguished himself at Oudenarde (1708) and Malplaquet. Became a General in 1712 and a Field-Marshal in 1742.

ST CLAIR, Arthur (c.1734-1818) of Thurso. Soldier and General. As a Lieutenant under General Wolfe he carried the colours on the Plains of Abraham. Sometime adviser to General Washington. Was elected President of Congress and Government of North West Territories.

STEEL, David Martin Scott (1938-) of Buckhaven, Fife. Journalist, broadcaster and politician. Was leader of the Liberal Party from 1976 to 1987.

STEELE, Sir John (1804-91) of Aberdeen. Sculptor. His best work, the equestrian statue of the *Duke of Wellington* (1832) and that of *Prince Albert* (1876) in Edinburgh.

STEPHEN, Robert A. (1907-) educ. Aberdeen. Major-General (1961), Director of Army Surgery and Consulting Surgeon to the Army, RAMC College (1959-67).

STEPHENS, Joseph Rayner (1805-79) of Edinburgh. Social reformer. Made his name as a factory reformer. He was imprisoned for his struggle for the Ten Hours Act (1847).

STERLING, John (1806-44) of Kames Castle, Bute. Writer and noted contributor to *The Times*. In 1838 he founded the Sterling Club, among whose members were Carlyle, Allen Cunningham, Tennyson and Venables.

STEVENSON, Dorothy Emily (1892-1973) of Edinburgh, cousin of R. L. Stevenson. Author of novels and children's verse. Her best known novels incl. *Mrs Tim of the Regiment* (1932) and several other Mrs Tim books.

STEVENSON, Robert (1772-1850) of Glasgow. Builder of Lighthouses (incl. Bellrock). Invented the flashing system. He built 23 Scottish lighthouses, and was also a consulting engineer for roads, bridges, canals, harbours and railways. He was the grandfather of R. L. Stevenson.

STEVENSON, Robert Louis Balfour (1850-94) of Edinburgh. Novelist and poet. His romantic thriller *Treasure Island* (1883) was his most famous. *Kidnapped* (1886), *The Master of Ballantrae* (1889), *Catrina* (1893) and many others were and still are very popular.

STEVENSON, Robert S. (1889-1967) of Edinburgh. Consultant Ear, Nose and Throat Surgeon, Colonial Hosp., Gibraltar (1954-). Lecturer in Chicago (1948), Toronto (1952), Bristol (1955), London (1956), Philadelphia (1957) and Yale Univ. (1958).

STEVENSON, Thomas (1818-87) of Edinburgh. Constructor of lighthouses, with his father Robert and brother David. Lighting methods was his particular interest. He invented the Thermometer Screen which carries his name.

STEWART, Alexander B. (1908-) educ. Broughty-Ferry. Physician. Became Medical Adviser to the Greater London Council in 1965.

STEWART, Alexander D. (1883-1969) of Blairgowrie. Sometime Director of All India Institute of Hygiene, Calcutta.

STEWART, Alfred (1880-1947) of Glasgow. Scientist and writer of detective stories. Sometime Professor of Chemistry at Queen's Coll., Belfast. His stories incl. *Murder in the Maze, The Case with Nine Solutions* and *The Boat House Riddle.*

STEWART, Andy (1933-) of Glasgow. Composer, comedian and broadcaster. Became popular as host on TV's show *The White Heather Club.* His recording of 'A Scottish Soldier' sold about half a million copies.

STEWART, Dugald (1753-1828) of Edinburgh. Scholar and philosopher. Professor of Moral Philosophy. His works incl. *Elements of the Philosophy of the Human Mind* (3 vols. 1792-1817), and *View of the Active and Moral Powers of Man* (1828).

STEWART, Francis Teresa, Duchess of Richmond and Lennox (1647-1702), daughter of Lord Blantyre. Described by Pepys as the greatest beauty he ever saw in his life. She posed for the effigy of Britannia on the coinage.

STEWART, Sir Houston (1791-1895) of Ardgowan. Appointed Admiral of the Fleet in 1872.

STEWART, Sir Iain (1916-) of Glasgow. Directorships in Beaverbrook Newspapers Ltd., BEA, Eagle Star Ins. Co. Ltd., Royal Bank of Scotland Ltd., Lyle Shipping Co. Ltd. and British Caledonian Airline. He resigned BEA in 1974.

STEWART, James (Changed his name to Stewart Granger) (1913-) born in London, son of a Scottish army major, James Stewart. Actor. Achieved worldwide fame by his many starring roles in films such as *The Man in Gray, Madonna of the Seven Moons, Waterloo Road, Saraband for Dead Lovers, Adam and Evelyn, Young Bess, The Prisoner of Zenda, Beau Brummell, Bhowani Junction* and *Harry Black and the Tiger.*

STEWART, John Innes Mackintosh, born 1906 near Edinburgh. Scholar and detective story writer. Appointed in 1935 to the Chair of English at Adelaide University. His detective stories were written under the pseudonym 'Michael Innes' and the most successful included *Seven Suspects* (1936), *Lament for a Maker* (1939), *A Comedy of Errors* (1940) and *The Man from the Sea* (1955).

STEWART, John (Jackie) Young, born 1939 at Milton, Dunbartonshire. Grand Prix motor racing driver. World champion 1969, '71 and '73. Runner up 1972. Retired from motor racing in 1973.

STEWART, Roderick (Rod) David (1945-) born in London of Scottish parents, Super star entertainer and the most enduring of 'Pop' stars.

STEWART, Sir William (1774-1827) of Galloway. Soldier, became Lieut.- General and served with distinction under Wellington.

STEWART, William Ross (1889-1966) of Edinburgh. Major-General. Surgeon to the Viceroy of India (1933-36). Deputy Director Medical Services, Ceylon Command HQ (1942-44) and to North Command, India (1945-46).

STIRLING, James Hutchison (1820-1909) of Glasgow. Idealist, philosopher and lecturer. His *Secret of Hegel* (1865) introduced that Philosopher's system into Britain and was a masterly exposition.

STIRLING, Dr Robert (1790-1878) of Methven, Perthshire. Invented a type of gas-sealed internal combustion engine in 1817. Currently being re-examined by engineers in Britain, Holland and America in connection with the development of a low pollution engine.

STIRLING, William (1851-1932) of Grangemouth. Professor of

Physiology and History, Victoria Univ., Manchester. Sometime Professor of Physiology, Royal Institute of London.

STIRLING-ANSELAN, John E. (1875-1936) of Stirlingshire. Admiral. Served in China during the Boxer Rising (1900). Admiral Superintendent Chatham Dockyard (1927-31).

STIRLING-MAXWELL, Sir William (1818-78) of Glasgow. Historical writer, critic and virtuoso. Was the first British collector to buy Spanish paintings of the sixteenth and seventeenth centuries.

STOUT, Sir Robert, (1844-1930) of Shetland Isles. Member of Legislative Council of New Zealand (1926-30). Chief Justice of New Zealand (1899-1926).

STOW, David (1793-1864) of Paisley. Pioneer of coeducation. Advocated the mixing of sexes and the abolition of prizes and corporal punishment in schools.

STRACHAN, Douglas (1875-1950) of Aberdeen. Artist. Political cartoonist for the *Manchester Chronicle* (1895-97). He designed the windows for the shrine of the Scottish National War Memorial, Edinburgh. Goldsmith's Window in St Paul's Cathedral was also by him.

STRACHAN, John (1778-1867) of Aberdeen. Minister, became the first Bishop of Toronto in 1839.

STRANG, William (1859-1921). Painter and illustrator. Was an etcher of world class.

STRANGE or Strang, Sir Robert (1721-92) of Kirkwall, Orkney. Line engraver with a European reputation. He was made a member of the Academies of Rome, Paris, Florence, Bologna and Palma (1760-65).

STRATH, Sir William born 1909, educ. Glasgow. Sometime Chairman British Aluminium Co. Ltd., and several other Companies. Served in the Min. of Aircraft Production, Min. of Supply, and the Treasury (1940-55). Member of Atomic Energy Auth. (1955-59) and Permanent Sec. Min of Aviation (1959-69).

STRATHALMOND, (William Fraser) 1st Baron of Pumpherston (1888-1970). Chairman of British Petroleum Co. Ltd. (1941-56), Director Burmah Oil Co. Ltd., and National Provincial Bank Ltd., etc.

STRATHCLYDE, (Thomas D. Galbraith) 1st Baron of Barskimming, born 1891. Under-Sec. of State for Scotland (1945 and 1951-55). Chairman North of Scotland Hydro-Elect. Bd. (1959-).

STRATHCONA, (Donald Alexander Smith) 1st Baron (1820-1914) of Morayshire. Canadian Statesman. Chief promoter of the Canadian

Pacific Railway (1885). High Commissioner for Canada in London (1896).

STRATHNAIRN, (Hugh Rose) 1st Baron (1801-85), born in Berlin, soldier son of Scottish Diplomat, Sir George Rose. He virtually reconquered central India, and succeeded Lord Clyde as Commander in Chief, India (1860-65). He held the same post in Ireland (1865-70).

STUART, Sir Alexander (1825-86) of Edinburgh. Premier of New South Wales, Australia (1883-85).

STUART, Charles Edward Louis Philip Casimir (1720-88) known as the 'Young Pretender' and 'Bonnie Prince Charlie'. In 1745 he defeated the English under Cope, at Prestonpans, invaded England and marched as far south as Derby, but was later overwhelmed at Culloden by the Duke of Cumberland.

STUART, John, 3rd Earl of Bute (1713-92). First Scottish Prime Minister of Great Britain (1762-63).

STUART, John McDougall (1815-66) of Dysart, Fife. Engineer, surveyor and explorer in central Australia. Made six expeditions into the interior (1858-62). With Wm. Landsborough were the first to cross Australia from south to north. Mount Stuart is named after him.

SUTHERLAND, Alexander (1852-1902) of Glasgow. Australian journalist. Mathematical master in the Scotch College Melbourne (1875-77) and Principal of Carlton Coll., Melbourne (1877-92).

SUTHERLAND, Donald (1835-1919) of Wick, Caithness. Known as 'The Hermit of Milford Sound' in New Zealand. Discovered Sutherland Falls (one of the world's highest) which bears his name at Milford Sound. Sometime served in Italy with the forces of Garibaldi.

SUTHERLAND, George A. (1891-1970) of New Deer, Aberdeenshire. Physicist. Principal of Dalton Hall, Univ. of Manchester (1924-58). Lecturer on Physics in London and South Africa.

SUTHERLAND, Sir Gordon, born 1907 in Watten, Caithness. Professor of Physics at Univ. Coll., Michigan (1949-55). Master of Emmanuel Coll. Cambridge from 1964.

SUTHERLAND, Sir Iain (1925-86) son of a Wick-born artist. Diplomat. British Ambassador in Moscow (1982-85). His previous postings included Belgrade, Havana, Washington, Djakarta and Greece.

SUTHERLAND, James (1849-1905) born in Canada, son of Alexr. Sutherland of Caithness. Became Minister of Public Works in Canada.

SUTHERLAND, John (1808-91) of Edinburgh. Promoter of sanitary science. Was sent to Crimea in 1855 to investigate the sanitary conditions of British soldiers.

SUTHERLAND, Sir Thomas (1834-1922) of Aberdeen. Retired in 1914 as Chairman P & O Steam Navigation Co. and of the London Board of Suez Canal Co. Sometime Director of the London City and Midland Bank and Chairman, Marine and General Assurance Society.

SWAN, Annie Shepherd (Mrs D. C. Burnett) (1860-1943) from near Gorebridge. Novelist. Wrote *Aldersyde* (1883) and a great number of popular novels.

SWINBURNE, Sir James (1858-1958) of Inverness. Electrical engineer. Took out over 100 patents during his lifetime. Was an accomplished musician and set two of Tennyson's poems to music. Elected Fellow of the Royal Society.

SWINTON, Alan Campbell. Scottish electrical engineer. In 1908 he suggested an electronic television system in an article in the scientific journal *Nature*. He proposed that the cathod-ray tube could be used not only as a receiver, it could also be used to transmit pictures.

SYME, David (1827-1908) of North Berwick. Became an Australian newspaper proprietor and economist.

SYMES, James (1799-1870) of Edinburgh. Famous surgeon in his day. Professor Clinical Surgery, wrote on pathology, stricture, fistula, incised wounds, etc. Discovered a method of dissolving rubber to produce a water-proofing solution. He did not patent the discovery which was later taken up by Charles Mackintosh in the manufacture of waterproof fabrics.

SYMINGTON, William (1763-1831) of Leadhills. Millwright and inventor. Built one of the first steamboats in 1788. It had two paddle wheels in the middle of the deck. He was the inventor of a horizontal double-acting steam engine which he patented and fitted in the tug *Charlotte Dundas* in 1801. Unfortunately he died in poverty in London.

# T

TAIT, Archibald Campbell (1811-82) of Edinburgh. Became Archbishop of Canterbury in 1869. He did much to extend and improve the organisation of the Church in the Colonies.

TAIT, Peter Guthrie (1831-1901) of Dalkeith. Mathematician, philosopher and physicist. Professor of Mathematics at Belfast (1854). Produced the first working thermoelectric diagram. Published many papers on scientific subjects.

TAIT, William (1792-1864). Publisher and founder of *Tait's Edinburgh Magazine* (1823-64), a literary and radical political monthly.

TANNAHILL, Robert (1774-1810) of Paisley. Weaver and poet. Best remembered for his 'Bonnie Woods O'Craigie Lea', 'Jessie the Flower O'Dumblane' and 'The Lass of Arrenteenie'.

TASSIE, James (1735-99) of Pollokshaws, Glasgow. Engraver and modeller. Famed for his paste and imitation gems. Was commissioned by Catherine the Great of Russia to supply her with some 15,000 items of imitation gems and cameos. The collection was put on exhibition to the general public before being sent to the Empress. He invented the white enamel composition which he used for his medallion portraits.

TAYLOR, Sir George (1904-) educ. Edinburgh. Director of the Royal Botanic Gardens, Kew (1956-71). Joint leader of the British Museum Expedition to Rowenzori and mountains of East Africa (1934-35) and to SE Tibet and Bhutan in 1938.

TAYLOR, Tom (1817-80). Scottish dramatist and editor born at Sunderland. From 1846 he wrote or adapted over 100 pieces for the stage. Secretary to the Bd. of Health (1850-72). Became editor of *Punch* in 1874.

TEDDAR, Arthur William, 1st Baron Teddar of Glenguin (1890-1967) of Glenguin, Stirlingshire. Marshal of the Royal Air Force. From 1940 he organised the Middle East Air Force with great success and later became Deputy Supreme Commander under Eisenhower. In 1950 he was made Chancellor of the Univ. of Cambridge and also a governor of the BBC.

TELFORD, Sir Thomas (1757-1834) of Eskdale, Langholm. Son of a shepherd. Stonemason and Civil Engineer. Builder of bridges, aqueducts, canals and docks. The Caledonian Canal and the Menai Suspension Bridge were perhaps his greatest works. Constructed some 1,000 miles of roads and over 130 bridges in 10 years. He was the first President of the Institution of Civil Engineers. He is buried in Westminster Abbey.

TEMPLETON, James (1802-) Scottish carpet manufacturer. Devised modification of Chenille velvet technique and applied it to pile carpets and furnishings. Founded a factory in Glasgow in 1839. Received first of several royal commissions from Queen Victoria for carpet. In 1850 other carpet manufacturers were licensed to use his invention.

TENNANT, Charles (1768-1838) of Ochiltree, Ayrshire. Pioneer chemical industrialist. Developed and manufactured a bleaching powder.

THOM, James (1910-) educ. Edinburgh. Director of Forestry for England (1963-65), Director of Research (1965-68).

THOMAS the RHYMER (Sir Thomas Learmont) or THOMAS RYMOUR of ERCELDOUNE. (c.1220-97) of Berwickshire. Seer and poet. Said to have predicted the death of Alexander III and the battle of Bannockburn. His prophecies were collected and published in 1603.

THOMPSON, Sir D'Arcy Wentworth (1860-1948) of Edinburgh. Marine biologist and zoologist. His *Study in Growth and Form* (1917) had considerable merit. Other works include papers on fishing and oceanography. He was the leader of the 'Challanger' expedition.

THOMSON, Sir Adam of Glasgow. Airline pilot, founder and chairman of British Caledonian Airways (1972-87) then Britain's largest private airline.

THOMSON, Alexander (1817-75) of Glasgow. Distinguished architect who became known as 'Greek Thomson'.

THOMSON, Sir Charles Wyville (1830-82) of Bonsyde, West Lothian. Zoologist. Held professorships in Natural History at Cork, Belfast and Edinburgh. Famous for his deep-sea researches, described in *The*

*Depths of the Oceans* (1872). Elected FRS in 1867. Was head of the 1872-76 'Challanger' expedition. One of the first marine biologists to describe life in the ocean depths.

THOMSON, David (1912-) of Edinburgh. Professor of Public Law and Government, Columbia Univ., New York (1950-53) and member of the Institute for Advanced Study (1950) at Princeton. Became Master of Sidney Sussex Coll., Cambridge in 1957.

THOMSON, George (1757-1851) of Limekilns. Collector of Scottish songs and music and friend of Robert Burns. His *Collection of Scottish Songs and Airs* was produced in 5 Vols (1799-1818).

THOMSON, James (1700-48) of Ednam, Roxburghshire. Poet and playwright. A poet who had considerable influence on his contemporaries. His best known work is 'Rule Britannia' (1740).

THOMSON, James (1822-92) Scottish engineer born at Belfast and brother of Lord Kelvin. He was an authority on hydraulics, invented a turbine, and discovered the effect of pressure on the freezing point of water. Wrote papers on elastic fatigue, undercurrents and trade winds.

THOMSON, James (1834-82) of Port Glasgow. Poet of very considerable merit. Son of a sailor. 'City of Dreadful Night' was his greatest work. Others included 'Essays and Fantasies' (1881) and 'A Voice from the Nile' (1882).

THOMSON, John (1778-1840) of Dailly, Ayrshire. Divine and painter who was one of the first landscape painters in Scotland. Was greatly admired by Sir Walter Scott who described him as one of the warmest-hearted men living.

THOMSON, John (1837-) of Edinburgh. Pioneer photographer. One of the first great documentary photographers. Travelled and explored the Far East for ten years from 1862. His camera recorded kings and peasants, Court ceremonies and scenes of daily life, palaces, temples and monasteries. He also became photographic instructor to the Royal Geographical Society.

THOMSON, Sir John Arthur (1861-1933) of Palmuir, East Lothian. Naturalist. Published many popular works, some of the best known being, *The Wonder of Life, Outline of Science* and *Scientific Riddles. Outline of Biology* (1930) and *Biology for Every Man* (1933) were also his work.

THOMSON, Joseph (1858-95) of Penpont, Dumfriesshire. Geologist and explorer in Tanganyika (1878-79) and Masai country in Kenya (1883-84). Explored Southern Morocco for the Geographical Society in

1888. The Thomson Gazelle and Thomson Falls in Kenya bear his name.

THOMSON, Sir Joseph John (1856-1940). Born near Manchester, son of a Scottish antiquarian bookseller. Physicist who discovered the Electron in 1897. Nobel Prize winner for Physics in 1906.

THOMSON, Robert William (1822-73) of Stonehaven. Civil Engineer and expert on blasting. He was also an inventor. Designed improved machinery for making sugar in Java, invented a mobile steam crane and in 1845 the first pneumatic rubber tyre, but it was considered a curiosity and not developed, India rubber being very expensive at that time. He was also the inventor of a dry dock and fountain pen.

THOMSON, Ronald B. (1912-) of Aberdeen. Air Vice-Marshal, Air Officer Admin., Flying Training Command, (1963-). AOC-RAF Gibraltar (1958-60), Scotland and Northern Ireland (1960-63). Member of the Queen's Bodyguard for Scotland.

THOMSON, Roy Herbert, 1st Baron of Fleet (1894-1976). Born in Toronto son of a Scottish barber. Newspaper and Television magnate. In 1959 became one of Britain's leading newspaper proprietors with the acquisition of the Kemsley Newspapers.

THOMSON, Thomas (1773-1852) of Crieff. Chemist. When making investigations into brewing and distillation, he invented the instrument known as Allan's Saccharometer.

THOMSON, Thomas (1817-78) of Glasgow. Surgeon and Naturalist. Discovered pectic acid in carrots.

THOMSON, Thomas D. (1911-) of Edinburgh. Retired as Commissioner for Social Development, Nyasaland in 1963. Conducted a survey of adult education there (1956-57), and organised Nyasaland Council of Social Service (1959).

THORBURN, Archibald (1860-1935) Scottish artist who specialized in wildlife paintings. Exhibited at the Royal Academy (1880-1900).

THORNTON, Robert Campbell (1924-) of Leith. Appointed chief executive of the Debenham's Group in 1974 and Chairman in 1980. At the time there were 67 Debenham stores in the UK.

TODD, Sir Alexander Robustus, 1st Baron of Trumpington (1907-) of Glasgow. Biochemist. Professor at Manchester (1938) and at Cambridge (1944). Nobel prize winner for his researches on vitamins B and E. Elected FRS in 1942. Sometime described as the most eminent Scots scientist since Lord Kelvin. Was honoured by the Russians for outstanding achievements in organic chemistry.

TODD, Ruthven (1914-) of Edinburgh. Poet essayist and novelist. His first novel *Over the Mountain* (1939) was followed by *The Lost Traveller* (1943) and *The Ruins of Time* in 1950.

TROTTER, Alexander (Sandy) C. (1902-75) of Edinburgh. Editor of the *Scottish Daily Express* (1934-59) and Chairman of Beaverbrook Newspapers (1959-70).

TROUP, Sir James A.V. (1883-) of Broughty Ferry. Vice-Admiral (1939), Rear-Admiral, Director of Naval Intelligence (1935-39).

TULLOCH, John (1823-86) of Bridge of Earn. Theologian. Principal and Professor of Divinity at St Mary's Coll., St Andrews. He was the founder of the Scottish Liberal Church Party in 1878.

TURNBULL, Sir Hugh Stevenson (1882-1973). Educ. Edinburgh. Was the Commissioner of Police for the City of London (1925-50).

TURNER, Sir William (1907-) of Kelso. Lieut.-General (1956). OC 5th and later 1st KOSB (1942-46). GSOI, Middle East and Gt. Britain (1947-50). GO C in C, Scottish Command, and Governor of Edinburgh Castle (1961-64). Member of the Queen's Bodyguard for Scotland (The Royal Company of Archers).

TWEED, John (1869-1933) of Glasgow. Sculptor. Among his principal works are the *Cecil Rhodes* memorial at Bulawayo, the completion of Steven's *Duke of Wellington* at St Paul's and *Clive* in Whitehall.

TWEEDSMUIR, (John N. S. Buchan), 2nd Baron of Elsfield, (1911-). Served with distinction in the Canadian army (1939-45). President, Commonwealth and British Empire Chamber of Commerce (1955-57). President, Institute of Export (1963-).

TWEEDSMUIR, Priscilla J. F. Buchan, Baroness (life peeress) of Belhelvie. From Potterton, Aberdeen. Member of State at the Foreign Office. Leader of Delegation to Iceland on fishing limits dispute (1972-). Was UK Delegate to UN General assembly (1960-61).

TYTLER, (1) William of Woodhouselee (1711-92) of Edinburgh. Historian, lawyer and writer to the signet. *An Inquiry into the Evidence against Mary Queen of Scots* (1759) was his work.

TYTLER, (2) Alexander Fraser (1749-1813), Historian son of (1) above. Became Judge Advocate for Scotland in 1790, and a Judge of Session (1802) as Lord Woodhouselee.

TYTLER, (3) Patrick Fraser (1791-1849), son of (2) above. Published *A Critical History of Scotland 1249-1603* (1828-43) which is still valuable.

# U

URE, Andrew (1778-1857) of Glasgow. Sometime Prof. of Chemistry and Natural Philosophy at Anderson's College, and Analytical Chemist to the Board of Customs, London (1834). Produced a *Dictionary of Chemistry* (1821). Was the inventor of the Alkalimeter (1816) and a Bi-metal thermostat in 1830. Elected FRS in 1822.

URE, David (?-d.1798) of Glasgow. Geologist. Was employed by Sir John Sinclair in his preparation of the *First Statistical Account of Scotland.*

URE, Mary (1934-75) of Glasgow. Actress. Played leading parts in many films and on Television. Her films include, *Look Back in Anger, Sons and Lovers, Where Eagles Dare* and *The Mindbenders.* TV appearances include *Honour thy Father and thy Mother.*

URQUHART, David (1805-77) of Cromarty. Diplomat, writer and politician. Founded the *Free Press* afterwards called *Diplomatic Review.* Wrote *The Pillars of Hercules* (1850) in which he suggested the introduction of Turkish Baths into Britain.

URQUHART, Robert (1922-) of Ullapool. Actor with numerous appearances on stage, film and radio. Films Inc., *Only Young Twice, Knights of the Round Table* and *The Curse of Frankenstein.*

URQUHART, Sir Robert W. (1896-) educ. Aberdeen. Appointed Inspector-General of HM Consular Establishments in 1945, Minister at Washington (1947), at Shanghai (1948-50) and Brit. Ambassador to Venezuela (1951-55).

URQUHART, Sir Thomas (1611-60) of Cromarty. Author and devoted warrior for Charles I and Charles II. Known for his brilliant translation *Rabelais.* Said to have died from a fit of laughter on hearing of the restoration of Charles II.

# V

VEITCH, John (1829-94) of Peebles. Author. Professor of Logic and Rhetoric at St Andrew's (1860). His works include *Tweed and other Poems* (1848), *Lives of Dugal Stewart* (1857) and *Sir W. Hamilton* (1869).

VEITCH, William (1794-1885) of Spittal near Jedburgh. Classical scholar. His chief work was the invaluable *Greek Verbs Irregular and Defective* (1848). Fourth edition in 1878.

VEITCH, William (1885-1968) of Edinburgh. Director of Kemsley Newspapers (1937-57).

VEITCH, William L.D. (1901-69) of Edinburgh. Major-General. Commanded the Bengal Sappers and Miners (1943-46). Was Engineer-in-Chief, Pakistan Army (1950-53).

# W

WADDELL, Sir Alexander (1913-) of Angus. Colonial Secretary, Gambia (1952-56), Sierra Leone (1956-58). Governor and C in C, Sarawak (1960-63).

WALKER, Sir James (1863-1935) of Dundee. Chemist. Known for his work on hydrolysis, ionization and amphoteric electrolytes. Elected FRS in 1900.

WALKER, James (1916-) educated Falkirk. Professor of Obstetrics and Gynaecology. Visiting Prof. Univ. of New York State (1957), Florida (1965) and McGill Univ. (1967).

WALLACE, Alfred Russel (1823-1913) of Usk, Monmouthshire and of Scottish descent. Architect, land surveyor and naturalist who independently formulated before Darwin, the theory of natural selection. Elected FRS in 1893.

WALLACE, Sir Donald Mackenzie (1841-1919) of Dunbartonshire. Journalist, and author. Traveller and foreign correspondent of *The Times*. Edited 10th edition of *Encyclopaedia Britannica*. Was private sec. to two Viceroys of India. Wrote his highly successful *Russia* in 1877.

WALLACE, Ian B. (1919-), born in London of Scottish (Kirkcaldy) parents. Singer, actor and broadcaster. Panellist on radio and TV quiz game *My Music*. Theatrical career includes a Royal Command Performance in the Palladium (1952) and 'Toad' in *Toad of Toad Hall* (1964).

WALLACE, John B. (1907-) of Cambuslang. Air Vice-Marshal. Deputy Director-General of Medical Services, RAF (1961-66).

WALLACE, Nellie (1870-1948) of Glasgow. Comedienne. Described as the funniest of all Scottish women comics.

WALLACE, Robert (1773-1855) of Ayrshire. Parliamentarian, Postal and Law reformer. It was mainly through him that Rowland Hill's Penny Postage was introduced.

WALLACE, Sir William (1274-1305) of Elderslie, Renfrewshire. Scottish patriot, hero and martyr. Chief champion of Scotland's independence. Routed the English at the battle of Stirling Bridge in 1297.

WALLS, Henry (1907-) of Edinburgh. Director, Metropolitan Police Laboratory, New Scotland Yard (1964-). Dir. Home Office Forensic Science Lab., Newcastle upon Tyne (1958-64).

WARDLAW, Henry (1378-1440). Scottish Divine who played a prominent part in founding St Andrews University (1411).

WATERS, Sir George Alexander (1880-1967) of Thurso, Caithness. Editor of the *Scotsman* (1924-44).

WATERSTON, John James (1811-83) of Edinburgh. Physicist. Developed the Kinetic theory of gases. Was the first to make an accurate theoretical prediction of the speed of sound.

WATSON, Benjamin P. (1880-) of Anstruther. Sometime professor of Obstetrics and Gynaecology, Columbia Univ., New York.

WATSON, Sir Daril G. (1888-1967) of Paisley ? General, GOC 2nd Div. (1940-41), Asst. Chief Imp. General Staff (1942), GOC in C Western Command (1944-46) and Quartermaster-General to the Forces (1946-47).

WATSON, Sir James A. S. (1889-1966) of Dundee. Agricultural Attaché, Brit. Embassy, Washington (1942-44). Chief Scientific and Agricultural Adviser to Min. of Agric., and Director-General, Nat. Agric. Advisory Service (1948-54).

WATSON, James W. (1915-), educ. Edinburgh and Toronto. Professor of Geography and Head of the Dept. of Geography, Edinburgh Univ. (1954-). Was Chief Geographer, Canada, and Director of the Geographical Branch, Dept. of Mines and Tech. Surveys, Canada (1949-54).

WATSON, John (1850-1907) born in Essex. Scottish novelist and minister. His pseudonym was 'Ian Maclaren'. His writings were popular for his descriptions of Scottish rural life, including *Beside the Bonny Brier Bush* (1894) and *The Young Barbarians* (1901).

WATSON, Robert (1746-1838) of Elgin. Adventurer. Fought for American Independence. Sometime Napoleon's tutor in English, and President of Scots College, Paris.

WATSON-WATT, Sir Robert Alexander (1892-1973) of Brechin. Physicist and inventor. Appointed Scientific Adviser to the Air Ministry in 1940. He was the inventor of Radar.

WATT, George Fiddes (1873-1960) of Aberdeen. Portrait painter. Became noted for his portraits of celebrated men of his time.

WATT, Harry (1906-) of Edinburgh. Film director. Some of his best known feature films included *Night Mail* (1936) *The Overlanders* (1946) and *Where no Vultures Fly* (1951).

WATT, James (1736-1819) of Greenock. Mathematical instrument maker and prolific inventor. Developed the improved steam engine, invented the condenser (1765), sun and planet gear (1784), the governor, water gauge, parallel motion, smokeless furnace and a letter copying machine. The 'Watt' as a unit of power is named after him.

WATT, Robert (1774-1819) of Stewarton, Ayrshire. Bibliographer and distinguished physician. Known for his *Bibliotheca Britannica* (1819-24).

WAUGH, Sir Andrew Scott (1810-78) educ. Edinburgh. Major-General and Surveyor-General of India (1843-).

WAUGH, Sir Arthur A. (1891-1968) of Edinburgh. Secretary, Dept. of Supply, Gov. of India (1943). Controller of Establishments, British Consul (1948-54), Chairman, Salaries Commission, Ghana (1956-57).

WAVERLEY, (John Anderson) (1882-1958) 1st Viscount of Eskbank. Administrator and Cabinet Minister. Home Sec. and Min. for Home Security (1939-40). The 'Anderson' air raid shelter bears his name. Became Chancellor of the Exchequer in 1943. He later introduced pay-as-you-earn income tax.

WEBSTER, John H.D. (1882-) of Edinburgh. Radiologist. Sometime Emeritus Consultant, Middlesex Hospital. Published several works on Periodicity in Nature, Life, Mind and Disease.

WEIR, James G. (1887-1973) of Dumfriesshire. Sometime Director of the Bank of England.

WEIR, Molly, of Glasgow. Character and Comedy actress and writer. Became popular on radio as Tattie McIntosh in *Itma*. Aggie in*Life with the Lyons* and Ivy McTweed in *The McFlannels*. She is the author of several and much enjoyed books.

WEMYSS, (Francis W. C. Douglas) (1818-1914) Earl of Wemyss, of Edinburgh. Politician and promoter of the volunteer system (1859 onwards) and the National Rifle Association.

WHITELAW, William Stephen Ian, 1st Viscount (1918-) of Monkland,

Nairn. Farmer and parliamentarian. His appointments incl. Chancellor
of the Exc. (1957-58), Lord President of Council and Leader of the
House of Commons (1972-73), Sec. of State for N. Ireland (1972-73),
Home Sec. (1979-83), Leader, House of Lords (1983-88).
WHEELER, Sir Robert Eric Mortimer (1890-1976) of Glasgow.
Archaeologist. Was Keeper and Secretary of the London Museum
(1926-34). Prof. of the Archaeology of the Roman Provinces at the
Univ. of London (1948-55). Served in the Army in both World Wars.
Commanded a Brigade in North Africa and Italy.
WHITTEN-BROWN, Sir Arthur (1886-1948) of Glasgow. Airman who
with Sir John Alcock made the first direct transatlantic flight in 1919 in
a Vickers Vimy bomber plane. He won a prize of £10,000.
WHYTT, Robert (1714-66) of Edinburgh. A pioneer neurologist. One
of the first to investigate reflex action.
WIGHT, James Alfred (1916-) of Glasgow. Veterinary surgeon. Best
known as the best selling author 'James Herriot'. His many works incl.
*If only they could Talk* (1970), *It Shouldn't Happen to a Vet* and *All
Creatures Great and Small* (1972), *Let Sleeping Vets Lie* and *All
Things Bright and Beautiful* (1973), *Vet in Harness* (1974), *Vets Might
Fly* (1976) and *Vet in Spain* (1977).
WILKIE, Sir David (1785-1841) of Cults in Fife. Painter and etcher.
Famous for such pictures as *The Blind Fiddler* (1806) and the *Village
Festival* (1811), both in the Tate Gallery. In 1830 he was made painter
extraordinary to the King. Elected RA in 1811.
WILKIE, David (1954-). Scotsman born in Colombo, Sri Lanka.
Swimmer and sports commentator. Olympic gold medal winner in 1976
in the 200 metres breaststroke. Held 30 major records (3 World, 9
European and 18 Commonwealth) and 15 major swimming medals (8
Gold, 4 Silver and 3 Bronze). Writer's Assoc of Gt. Britain 'Sportsman
of the Year' 1975 and Europe swimming 'Man of the Year' 1975.
WILLIAMSON, John (1740-1803) of Eshaness, Shetland. Weaver and
true pioneer in the fight against smallpox by serum inoculations. He
was also a blacksmith, carpenter and clock repairer. His frequent
dabbling in mechanical inventions earned him the nickname 'Johnnie
Notions'. His development of a serum against smallpox preceded
Englishman Edward Jenner's who was generally credited as being first
with successful inoculations.
WILSON, Alexander (1766-1813) of Paisley. Artist, Ornithologist and
poet. Went to America in 1794. His skill in drawing led him to paint a

collection of all the birds in America, and then published *American Ornithology* (1808-13 in 7 vols.)

WILSON, Arthur G. (1900-) of Glasgow ? Major-General GSOI Australian Imperial Forces, UK and later Asst. Military Liaison Officer, Aust. High Commissioner's Office UK till 1943. With Australian Forces in New Guinea, Philippines and Borneo (1943-45). Commanded the British Commonwealth Base, Japan (1946-47).

WILSON, Charles Thomson-Rees (1869-1959) of Glencorse. Pioneer in Atomic and Nuclear Physics. Prof. of Natural Philosophy at Cambridge (1925-34). Famous for his invention of the 'Wilson Cloud Chamber', an indispensible tool of modern physics ever since for which he was awarded the Nobel Prize for Physics in 1927. Elected a Fellow of the Royal Society.

WILSON, James (1805-60) of Hawick. Economist. Became an authority on the Corn Laws and Currency. Founded *The Economist*.

WILSON, James of St Andrews. A member of the US Constitutional Convention of 1787 and an Assoc. Justice of the US Supreme Court.

WILSON, John (nicknamed 'Christopher North') (1785-1858) of Paisley. Journalist and poet. Elected to the Chair of Moral Philosophy in Edinburgh in 1820.

WILSON, John (1800-49) of Edinburgh. Singer. For years a favourite operatic tenor in London (Covent Garden and Drury Lane). Toured America and Canada.

WILSON, John (1804-75) of Lauder. Missionary in Bombay (1828-75). Sometime Vice-Chancellor of Bombay University. Worked for abolition of the slave trade.

WILSON, John Mackay (1804-35) of Tweedmouth. Writer and editor. Known for his *Tales of the Borders* (6 vols. 1833-40) which was continued after his death by his widow.

WILSON, Robert (1803-82) of Dunbar. Inventor of the screw propellor for ships, and a double-acting steam hammer in 1861.

WILSON, Robert (-d.1964) Scottish singer who popularised the old song 'Scotland the Brave', now regarded by many as the Scottish Anthem.

WILSON, Samuel, born in America of Greenock parents. The original 'Uncle Sam' of America, and his wife was known as 'Aunt Betsy'. He was a meat packer, supplying the Colonial army in 1812.

WIMBERLEY, Douglas N. (1896-) Major-General Commanding the 51st Highland Div. (1941-43) in North Africa when Rommel was defeated at Alamein.

WISHART, George (c.1513-46) of Kincardineshire. Protestant reformer and martyr. Translated the Swiss *Confessions of Faith*. Was arrested at Cardinal Beaton's instance in 1546 and burned at St Andrews on a charge of heresy.

WITHERSPOON, Dr John (1723-94) from East Lothian. Theologian and Minister. Went to America and became first President of Princeton University. Was the only cleric to be one of the signatories of the American Declaration of Independence in 1776.

WOLFSON, Sir Isaac (1897-) of Glasgow. Became a chain stores tycoon, and head of The Great Universal Stores Ltd.

WOOD, Alexander (1817-84) Scottish physician who advocated the use of the Hypodermic Syringe for injections in 1883.

WOOD, Sir Andrew (c.1455-1539) of Largo. Naval Commander associated with James IV in his efforts to build up a Scottish Navy. Was very successful against English vessels raiding in the Firth of Forth.

WOODBURN, Arthur (1890-) of Edinburgh. Parliamentary Sec. Min. of Supply (1945-47). Sec. of State for Scotland (1947-50). Member, Select Committee on House of Commons Procedure (1956-68).

WRIGHT, Revd Ronald Selby (1908-) of Edinburgh? Broadcaster known as the 'Radio Padre'. Toured all Commands during World War II. Chaplain for the Queen in Scotland (1963-).

# Y

YATES, Edmund (1831-94) of Edinburgh. Journalist and novelist. In 1874 he founded with Granville Murray a successful society weekly *The World*. He published over 20 novels.

YOUNG, Andrew (1807-89) of Edinburgh. Schoolmaster, poet and hymn writer. 'There is a Happy Land' his best known hymn.

YOUNG, Andrew John (1885-1971) of Elgin. Clergyman and poet. Was Canon of Chichester Cathedral (1948-). His many nature poems incl. 'Boaz and Ruth' (1920), 'The Bird Cage' (1926), 'The White Blackbird' (1935), 'The Green Man' (1947) and 'Into Hades' (1952), He also published Botanical essays. Was awarded the Queen's Medal for Poetry in 1952.

YOUNG, Arthur P. (1885-) of Ayrshire? Founder and Vice-President, Institute of Works Managers. Chairman, Confederation of Management Assocs. (1938-48) and of Institute of Works Managers (1934-50).

YOUNG, James (1811-89) of Glasgow. Industrial chemist. His experiments (1847-50) led to the manufacture of paraffin oil and solid paraffin on a large scale from shale. Was the founder of the world's first Commercial Oil Works (1851). Was sometimes known as 'Paraffin Young'. He amassed a large fortune, and was a great friend and financial supporter of David Livingstone. Elected FRS in 1873.

YOUNG, Ruth, of Dundee. Prof. of Surgery, Delhi Medical Coll. (1916-17), Director, Maternity and Child Welfare Bureau, Indian Red Cross (1931-35). Adviser, Ethiopian Women's Work Assoc. on Welfare (1943).

YOUNG, Thomas (1587-1655) of Perthshire. Puritan Divine. Was

Milton's tutor till 1622. He later held charges in Hamburg and Essex.

YOUNG, Thomas (1893-) of Kilmarnock. Major-General (1949), Director of Medical Services, Far East Land Forces (1948) and Director, Army Health (1949-53). Retired 1953.

YULE, Sir Henry (1820-89) of Inveresk. Geographer, orientalist and author. Served in the Bengal Engineers (1840-62). Sat on the Indian Council (1875-87), Wrote *Cathay and the Way Thither* (1866) and a book on Marco Polo (1871). Attained distinction with others in the restoration and development of the irrigation system of the Moguls.

YULE, Joseph—better known as Mickey Rooney (1920-). His father was Joseph Yule of Edinburgh. Has been a famous Hollywood star actor from his early teens.

# Inventions and Discoveries

| | |
|---|---|
| ANDERSON, Adam | Measure of heights by barometer. |
| ANDERSON, James | Scotch plough. |
| ANDERSON, John | Balloon post, etc. |
| ARNOTT, Neil | Surgical and other appliances. |
| BAIN, Alexander | Chemical telegraph elect, clock, etc. |
| BAIRD, John Logie | Television. |
| BANKS, Donald | Rocket guidance system. |
| BARR, Archibald | Naval range finders. |
| BARTHOLOMEW, John G. | Discoveries in protozoology. |
| BEILBY, Sir George T. | Shale oil distillation, etc. |
| BELL, Alexander G. | Telephone. |
| BELL, Alexander M. | Visible speech. |
| BELL, Sir Charles | Sensory and motor nerve functions. |
| BELL, Revd Patrick | Mechanical reaper. |
| BLACK, Sir James | Betablockers. |
| BLACK, Joseph | Latent heat. |
| BLACK, Robert | Achromatic lenses for telescopes. |
| BLANE, Sir Gilbert | Prevention of Scurvy. |
| BREWSTER, Sir David | Kaleidoscope, etc. |
| BROWN, A. B. | Hydraulic steering for ships. |
| BROWN, Robert | Nucleus of living cells. |
| BROWN, Thomas | Scanner for viewing inside body. |
| BRUCE, Sir David | Sleeping sickness, etc. |
| BUCHAN, Alexander | Isobar system. |
| CAMERON, Charles | Soda water apparatus. |
| CAMPBELL, Angus | Cotton picking machine. |
| CHALMERS, James | Adhesive postage stamps. |
| CLERK, Sir Dugald | Two-stroke motor cycle engine. |
| CULLEN, William | Nervous system in health, etc. |
| CURRAN, Samuel | Scintillation detector. |

| | |
|---|---|
| CURRIE, James | Fibril diseases. |
| DAVIDSON, Robert | Electric locomotive. |
| DEWAR, Sir James | Vacuum flask, etc. |
| DRUMMOND, Thomas | Limelight. |
| DUNLOP, John B. | Pneumatic tyre. |
| ELPHINSTONE, Sir E. | Chart recorder, etc. |
| ELPHINSTONE, W. | Printing press. |
| FAIRBAIRN, Sir Wm. | Riveting machine. |
| FINLAYSON, James | Self-cleaning harrow. |
| FLEMING, Sir Alexr. | Penicillin. |
| FLEMING, Sir S. | Standard time. |
| FORBES, James D. | Light polarization. |
| FORBES, Sir John | Stethoscope. |
| FORSYTH, Alexr. J. | Percussion cap, etc. |
| GED, William | Stereotyping. |
| GILL, Sir David | Photography in astronomy. |
| GORDON, Sir Robert | Water pump. |
| GREGORY, David | Achromatic lenses. |
| GREGORY, James | Reflector telescope. |
| GREGORY, James | 'Gregorie's Mixture'. |
| HALL, Sir James | Experimental geology. |
| HARRISON, James | Refrigerator. |
| HENRY, Joseph | Electromagnetic induction. |
| HILL, David O. | Photography in portraiture. |
| HOLDEN, Sir Isaac | Lucifer match. |
| HORSBURGH, Thomas | Steel golf clubs. |
| ISAACS, Alick | Interferon. |
| JOHNSTON, John Lawson | Bovril. |
| KEILLER, Mrs | Marmalade. |
| KELVIN, Lord | Scientific instruments, etc. |
| KENNEDY, John | The Jack frame in spinning. |
| KERR, John | Magneto-optic effect. |
| LEIDHMAN, Sir Wm. B. | Vaccine against typhoid, etc. |
| LESLIE, Sir John | Differential thermometer. |
| LINDSAY, James B. | Electric light bulb. |
| LOW, Archibald M. | Radio signalling, etc. |
| MacADAM, John L. | Roads. |
| MacARTHUR, John | Vineyards in Australia. |
| MacEWEN, Sir William | Brain surgery. |

| | |
|---|---|
| MacKENZIE, Sir George | Identity of diamond with carbon. |
| MacKENZIE, Sir James | Polygraph. |
| McLAUCHLAN, John | 'Canada Dry' soft drinks. |
| MacLEOD, John J. R. | Isolation of insulin. |
| MacMILLAN, K. | Pedal cycle. |
| McNAUGHT, John | Compound steam engine. |
| MAIN, Alexr. | Fertilizer distributor. |
| MANSON, Sir Patrick | Parasites carried by insects. |
| MAXWELL, Jas. Clerk | Electromagnetic theory of light. |
| MEIKLE, Andrew | Threshing machine, etc. |
| MELVILLE, Thomas | Spectra of luminous gases. |
| MENZIES, Andrew | Coal cutting machine. |
| MENZIES, Michael | Threshing machine. |
| MILLAR, Patrick | Steam navigation. |
| MILLER, Maxwell | Still for spirits. |
| MONCRIEFF, Sir Alexr. | Gun pit system. |
| MUNRO, Alexander | Stomach tube. |
| MORRISON, Charles | Electric telegraph. |
| MORTON, Thomas | Patent slipway for ships. |
| MUIR, John | Self-setting sawmill, etc. |
| MURCHLAND, William | Milking machine. |
| MURDOCK, William | Gas Lighting, etc. |
| NAPIER, John | Logarithms. |
| NASMYTH, James | Steam hammer, etc. |
| NEILSON, James B. | Hot Blast in iron manufacture. |
| NICOL, William | Nicol prism. |
| RAMSAY, Sir William | Gases. |
| RILEY, James | Nickel steel. |
| ROPER, Andrew | Winnowing machine. |
| ROSS, Sir Ronald | Malaria parasite. |
| RUSSEL, John S. | Wave system in shipbuilding. |
| RUTHERFORD, D. | Carbon dioxide and max.-min. thermometer. |
| RUTHERFORD, E. | Atomic research. |
| SHIELDS, Alexr. | Milking machine. |
| SHIRRETT, Patrick | Cereal hybridizing. |
| SIMPSON, Sir James | Chloroform. |
| SINCLAIR, Daniel | Automatic telephone exchange. |
| SINCLAIR, (Earl) James | Steam carriage, etc. |

| | |
|---|---|
| SMALL, James | Swing plough. |
| SMITH, James | Thorough drainage. |
| STEVENSON, Robert | Lighthouse flashing systems. |
| STIRLING, Robert | Low pollution engine. |
| SYME, James | Waterproof solution. |
| SYMINGTON, William | Marine engines. |
| TAIT, Peter G. | Thermoelectric diagram. |
| TASSIE, James | Paste and imitation gems. |
| TEMPLETON, James | Chenille velvet technique. |
| TENNANT, Charles | Bleaching powder. |
| THOMSON, James | Hydraulics, etc. |
| THOMSON, Sir Robert J. | Electron. |
| THOMSON, Robert | Mobile steam crane, etc. |
| THOMSON, Thomas | Saccharometer. |
| THOMSON, Thomas | Pectic acid. |
| URE, Andrew | Alkalimeter, etc. |
| WATERSTON, J. J. | Kinetic theory of gases. |
| WATSON-WATT, Sir R. | Radar. |
| WATT, James | Steam engine, etc. |
| WHYTT, Robert | Reflex action. |
| WILSON, Charles | Wilson cloud chamber. |
| WILLIAMSON, John | Serum against smallpox. |
| WOOD, Alexander | Hypodermic. |
| YOUNG, James | Oil from shale. |

# Missionaries

| | |
|---|---|
| ANDERSON, John | Madras. |
| BURNS, William C. | China. |
| CHALMERS, James | New Guinea. |
| DUFF, Alexander | India. |
| FALCONER. I. K. | Middle East. |
| JOHNSTON, Dr James | Jamaica. |
| LEGGE, James | China. |
| LIVINGSTONE, David | Africa. |
| MacKAY, Alexr. M. | Uganda. |
| MILLER, William | India. |
| MILNE, William | China. |
| MILNE, Wm. (son of above) | China. |
| MORRISON, Robert | China. |
| MUIR, Ernest | Bengal. |
| PATON, John G. | New Hebrides. |
| PHILIP, Dr John | S. Africa. |
| SLESSOR, Mary | Africa. |
| WILSON, John | India. |

# Explorers

| | |
|---|---|
| BAIKIE, William B. | Niger River. |
| BENNETT, James | Congo. |
| BRUCE, James | Blue Nile, etc. |
| BRUCE, William | Antarctic, etc. |
| BURNES, Sir Alexr. | India. |
| CADELL, Francis | Australia. |
| CAMERON, V. L. | Africa. |
| CLAPPERTON, H. | Africa. |
| COOK, Capt. James | Australia, etc. |
| DOUGLAS, David | N. America. |
| GRANT, James A. | Africa. |
| JACK, Robert L. | Queensland. |
| LAING, Alexr. G. | Niger River. |
| LANDSBOROUGH, Wm. | Australia. |
| McCLINTOCK, Sir F. L. | Polar. |
| MacKAY, James | America. |
| MacKENZIE, Sir Alexr. | Canada. |
| MacKINNON, Quintin | New Zealand. |
| MITCHELL, Sir Thomas | Australia. |
| MUIR, John | America. |
| PARK, Mungo | Africa. |
| RAE, John | Arctic. |
| RICHARDSON, Sir John | Arctic. |
| ROSS, Sir James C. | Arctic. |
| ROSS, Sir John | Baffin Bay. |
| SELKIRK, Earl of | Red River. |
| SIMPSON, Sir George | Simpson's Falls, etc. |
| SIMPSON, Thomas | Simpson Strait, Canada. |
| STUART, John M. | Australia. |
| SUTHERLAND, Donald | New Zealand. |
| THOMSON, Joseph | Africa. |

# Prime Ministers and Premiers

| | |
|---|---|
| ABERDEEN, 4th Earl of | Great Britain. |
| BALFOUR, Arthur James | Great Britain. |
| CAMPBELL-BANNERMAN, Sir Henry | Great Britain. |
| DOUGLAS-HOME, Sir Alec | Great Britain. |
| FISHER, Andrew | Australia. |
| FRASER, Malcolm | Australia. |
| FRASER, Peter | New Zealand. |
| GLADSTONE, Wm. E. | Great Britain. |
| KIDSON, William | Australia. |
| LAW, A. Bonar | Great Britain. |
| MacALISTER, Arthur | Australia. |
| MacCULLOCH, Sir James | Australia. |
| McDONALD, Sir John (Premier) | Victoria, Australia. |
| MacDONALD, James Ramsay | Great Britain. |
| MacDONALD, Sir John A. | Canada. |
| MacILWRAITH, Sir Thomas (Premier) | Queensland, Australia. |
| MacKENZIE, Alexr. | Canada. |
| MacKENZIE, Sir Robert | Australia. |
| MacLEAN, Alan (Premier) | Victoria, Australia. |
| MacMILLAN, Harold | Great Britain. |
| MENZIES, Sir Robert | Australia. |
| NELSON, Sir Hugh M. (Premier) | Queensland, Australia. |
| REID, Sir G. H. | Australia. |
| STUART, Sir Alexr. (Premier) | N.S.W., Australia. |
| STUART, John, 3rd Earl of Bute | Great Britain. |